I0504166

Dinosaurs driving cars coloring pages for kids

EMILY WALKER

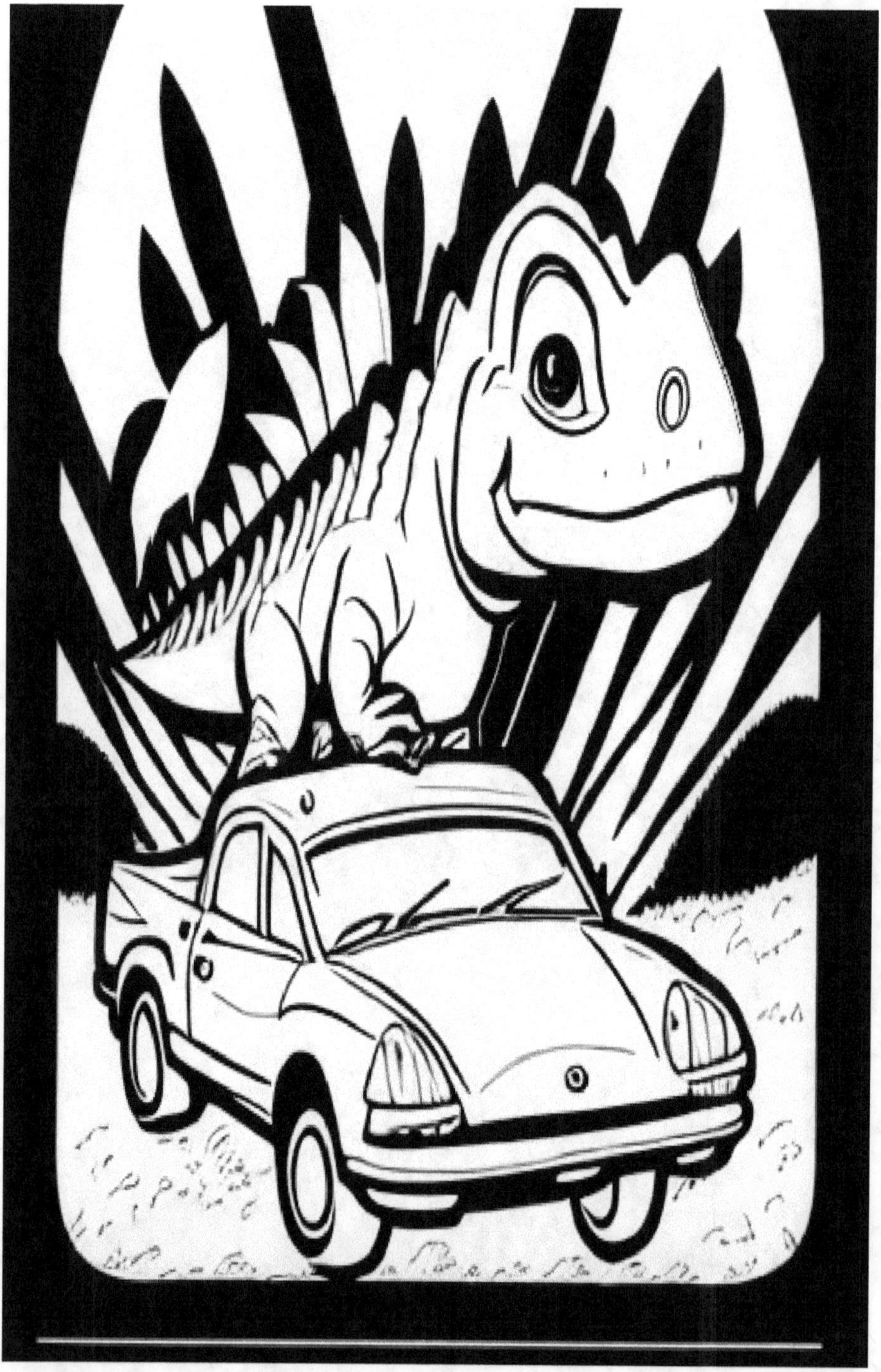

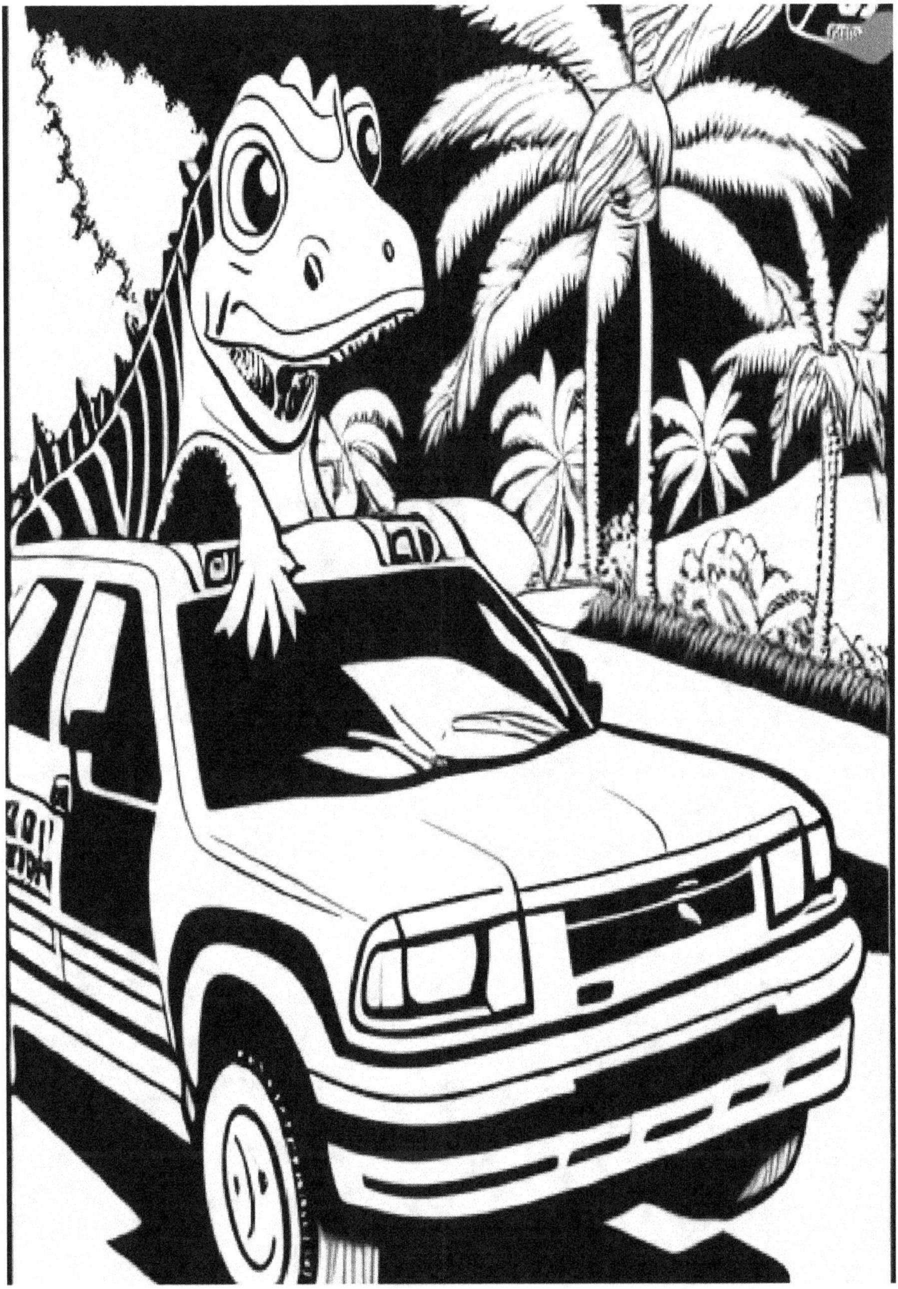

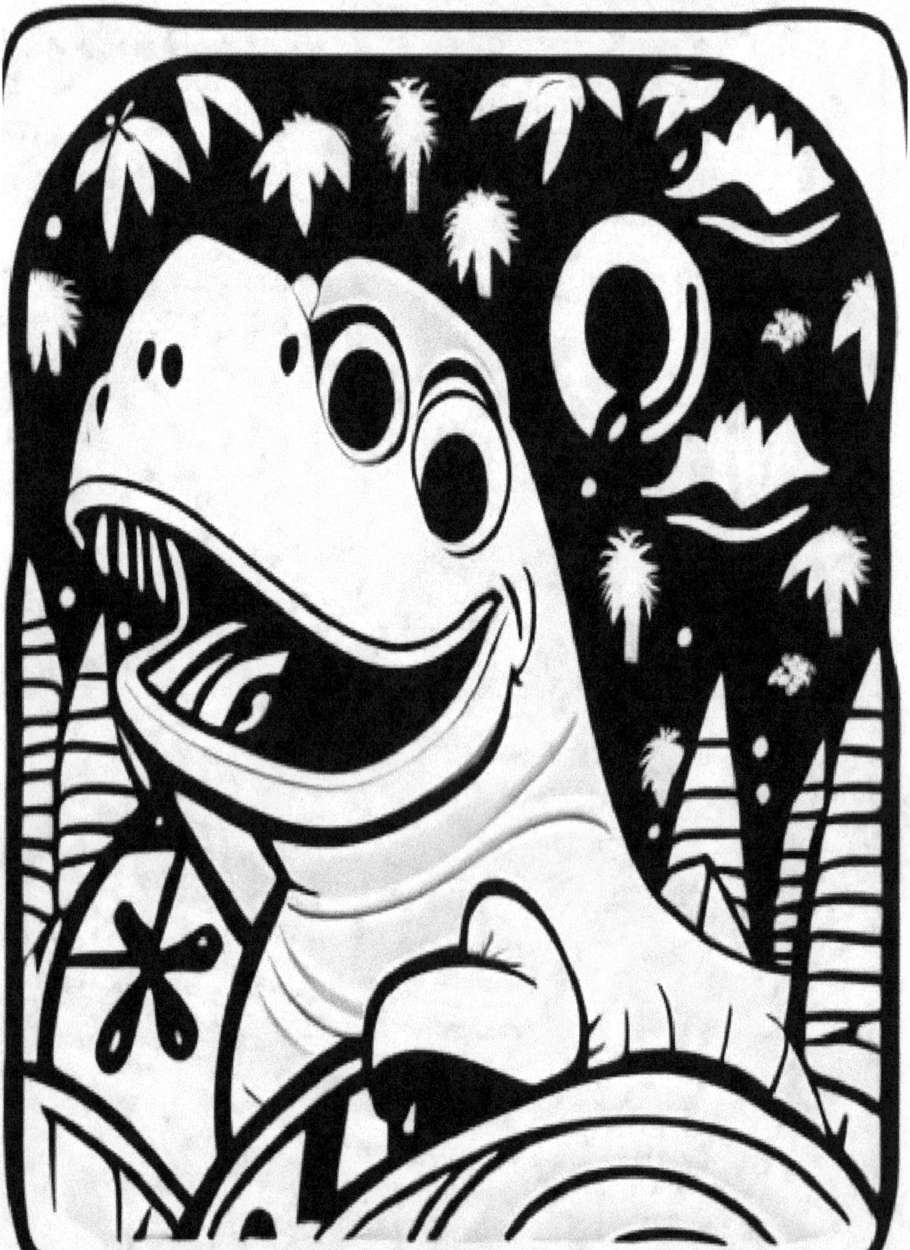

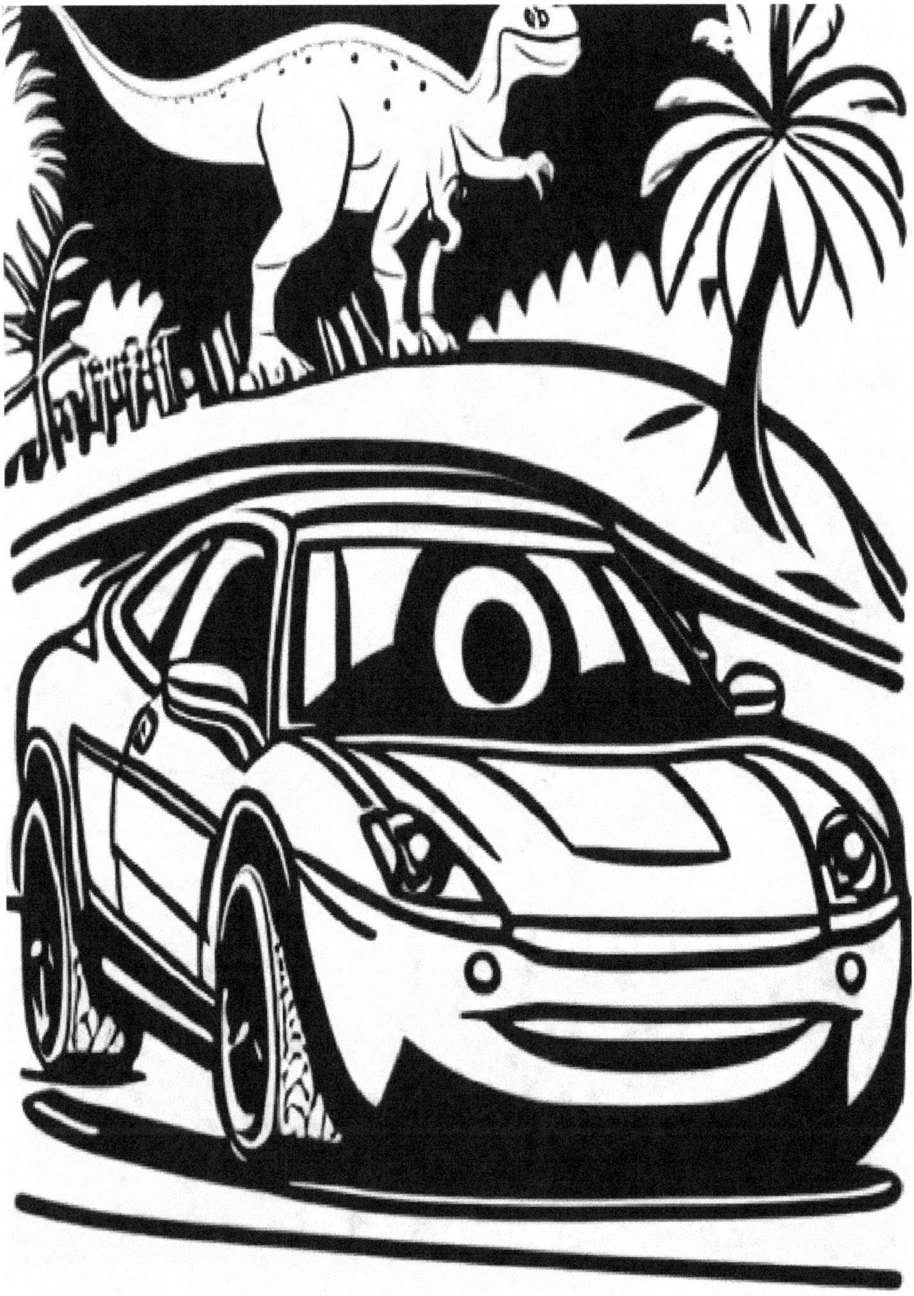

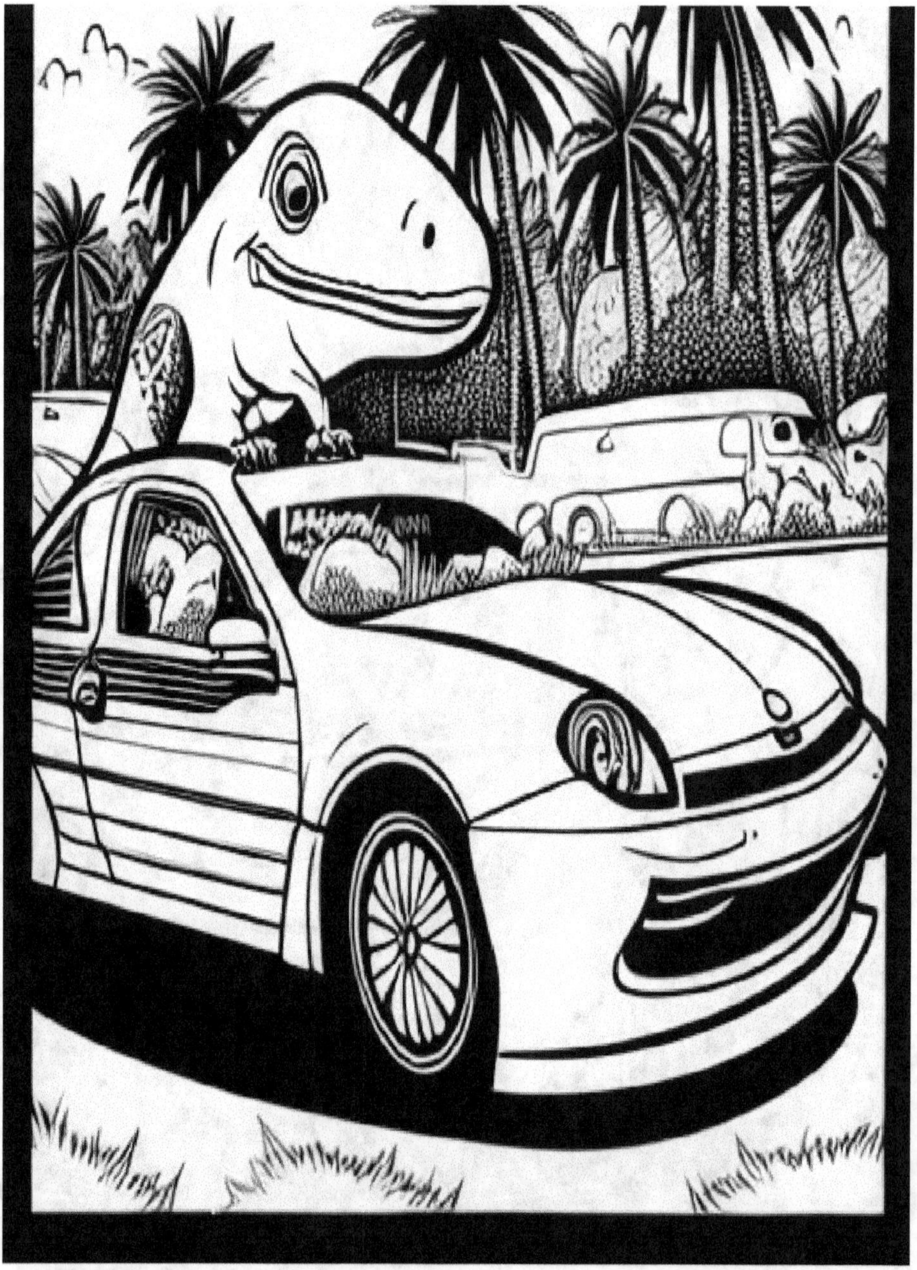

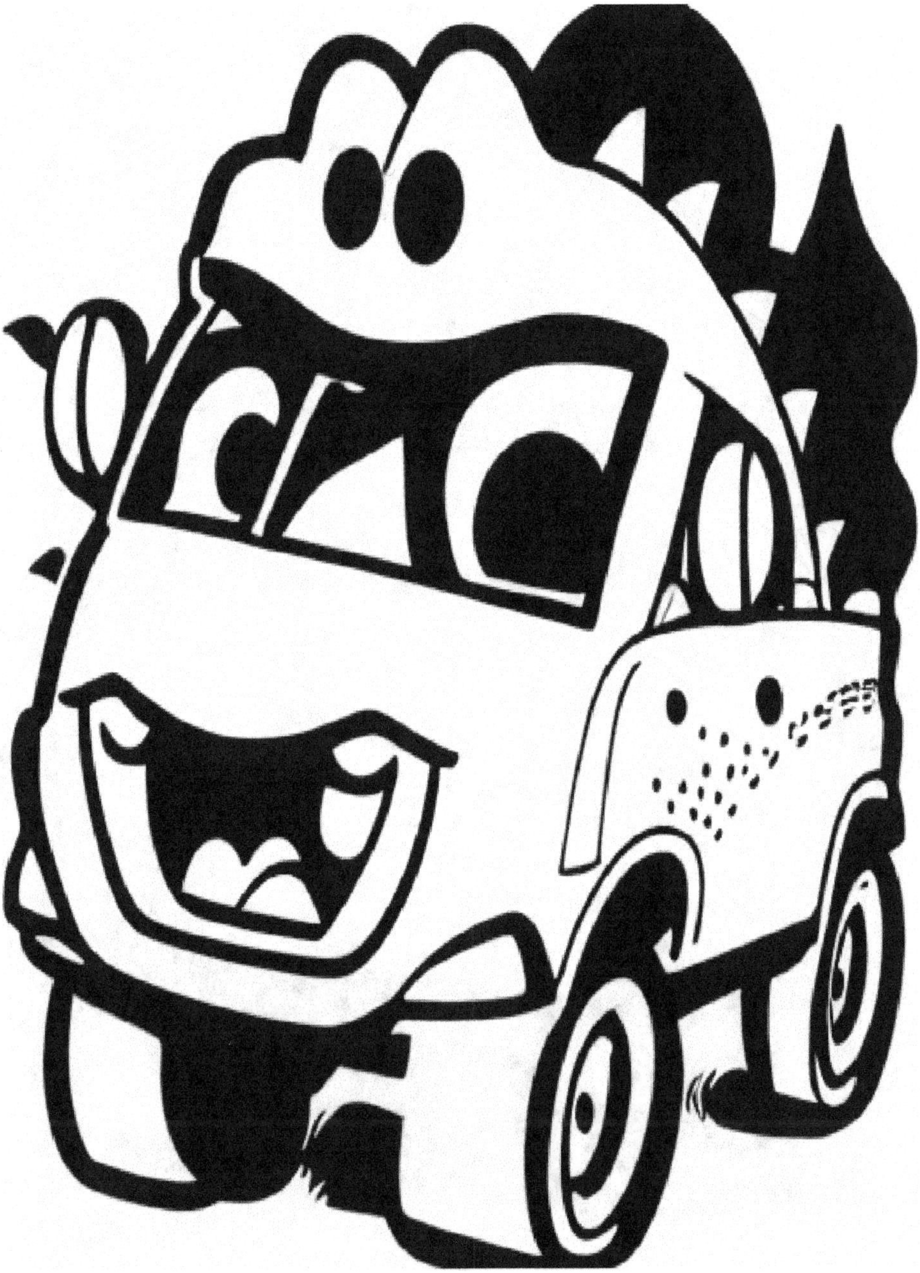

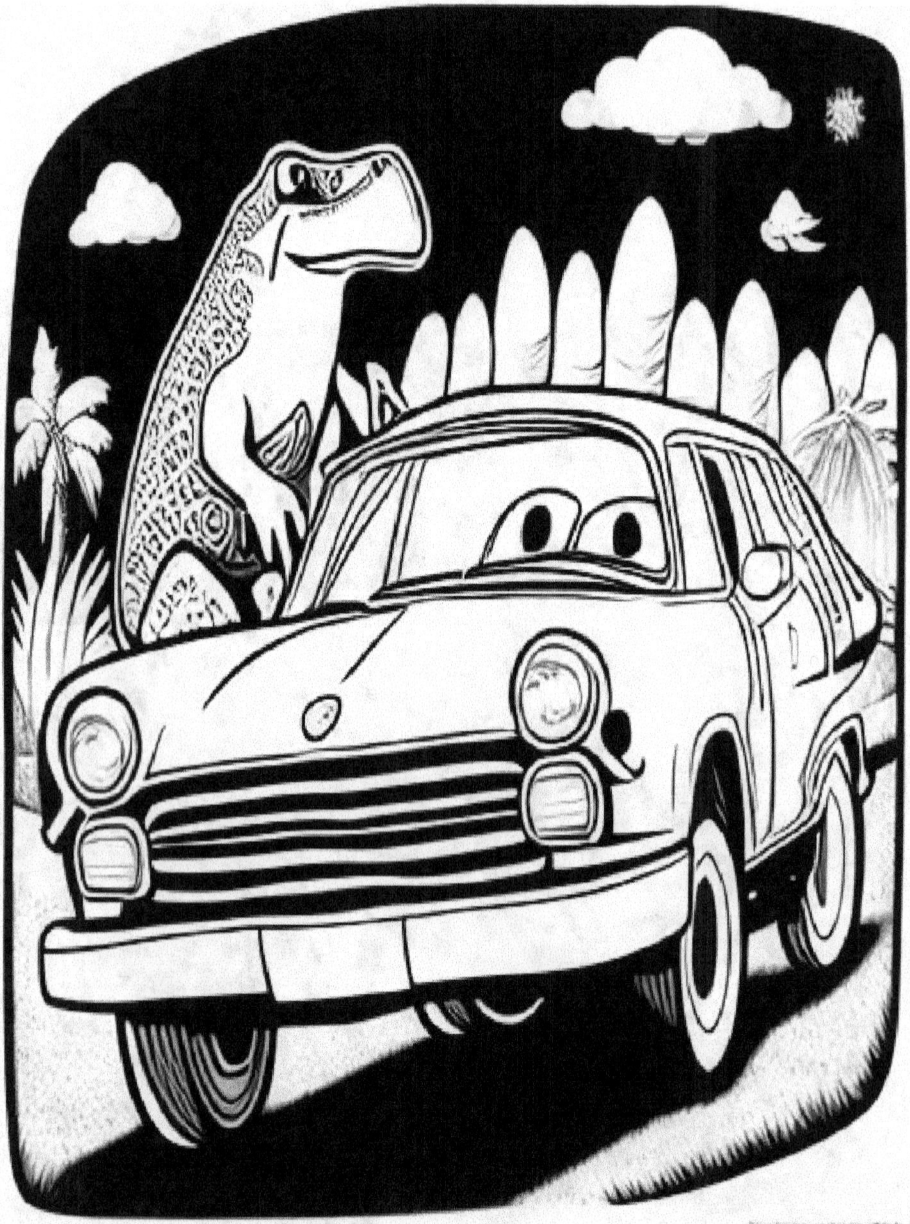

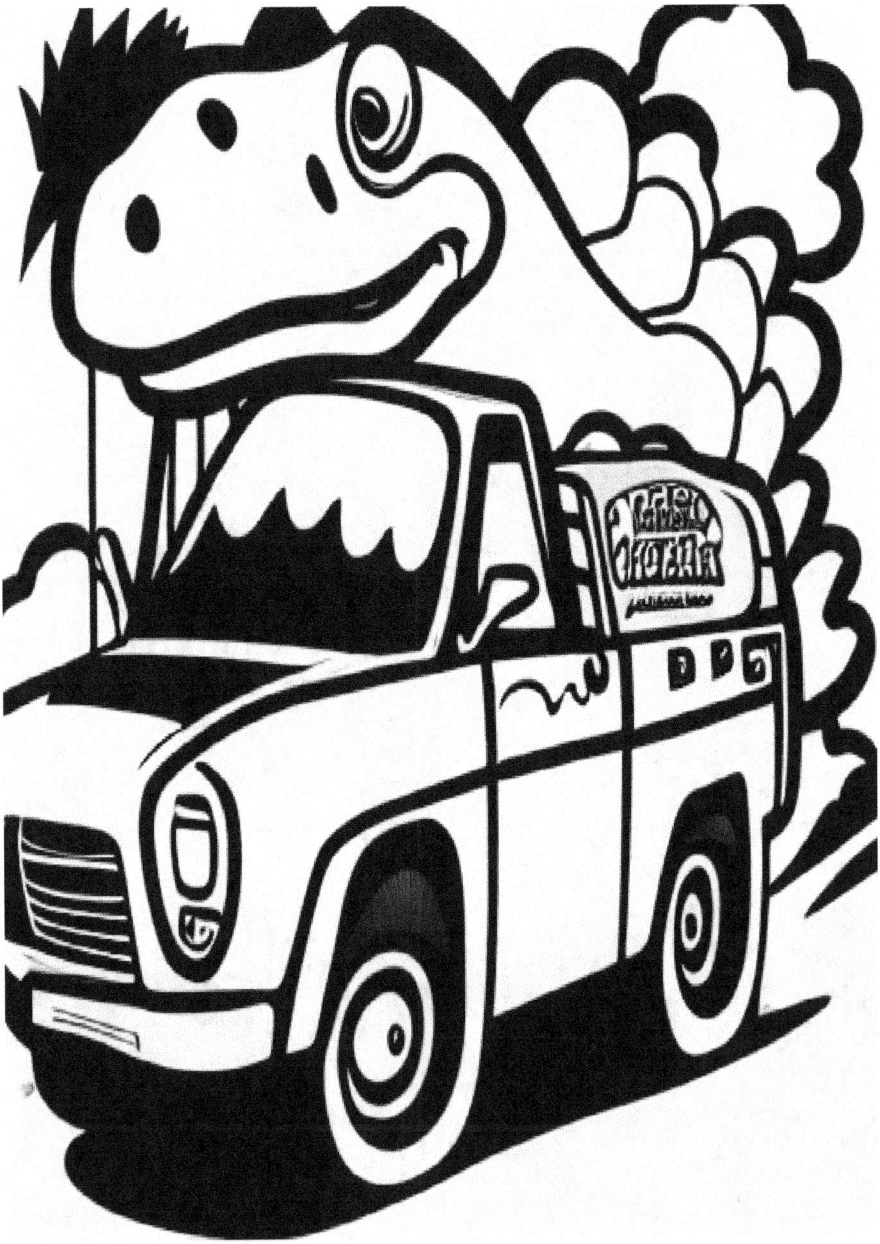

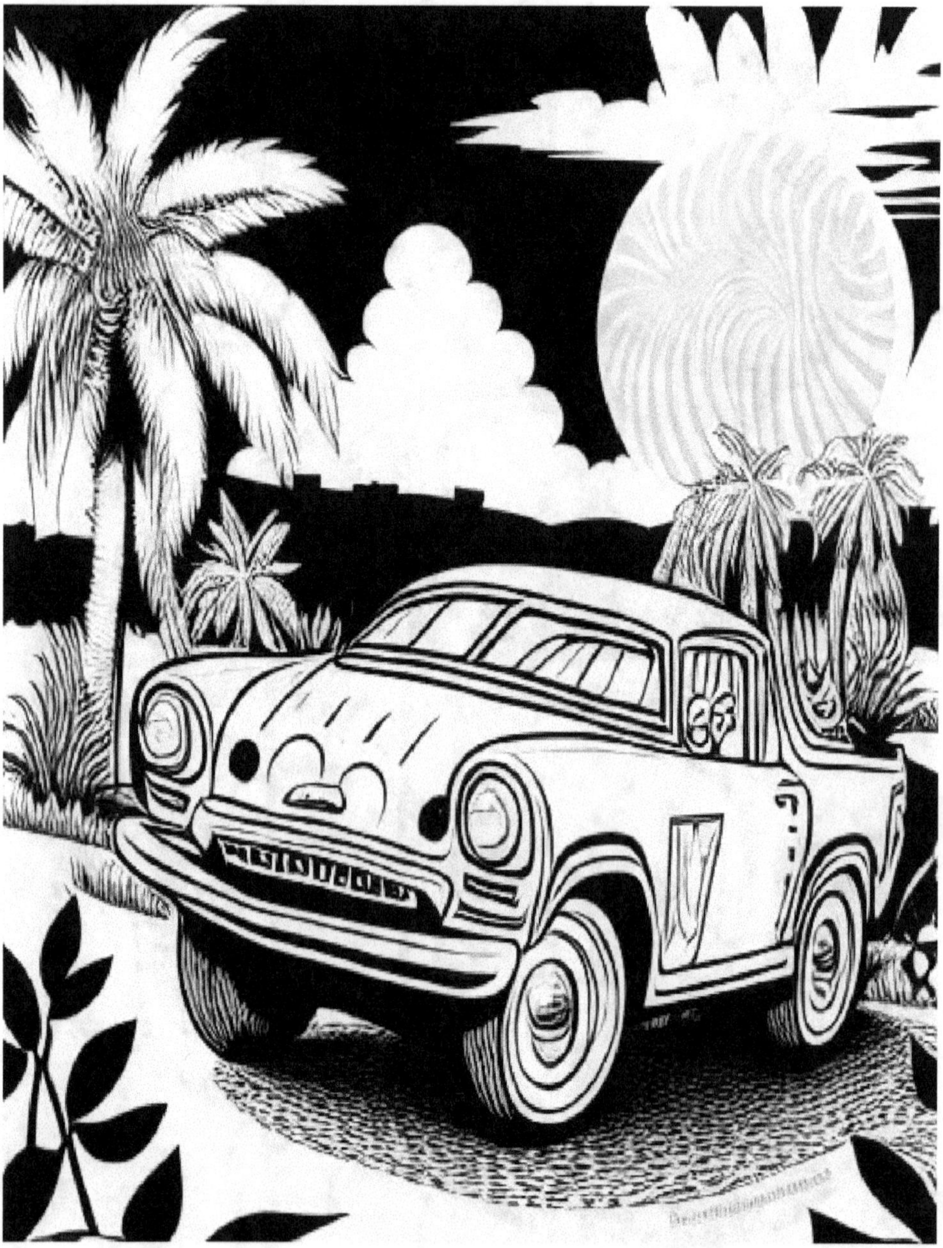

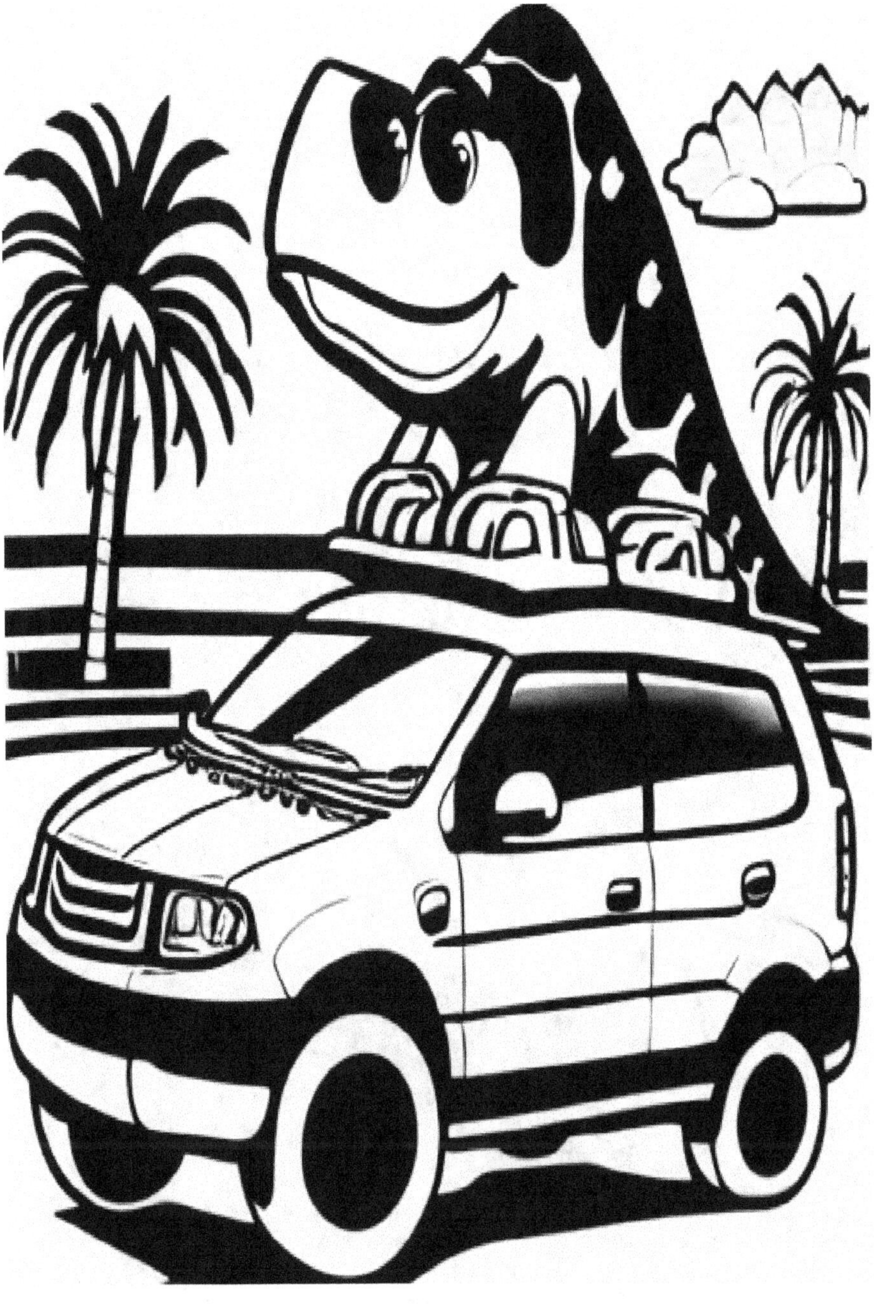

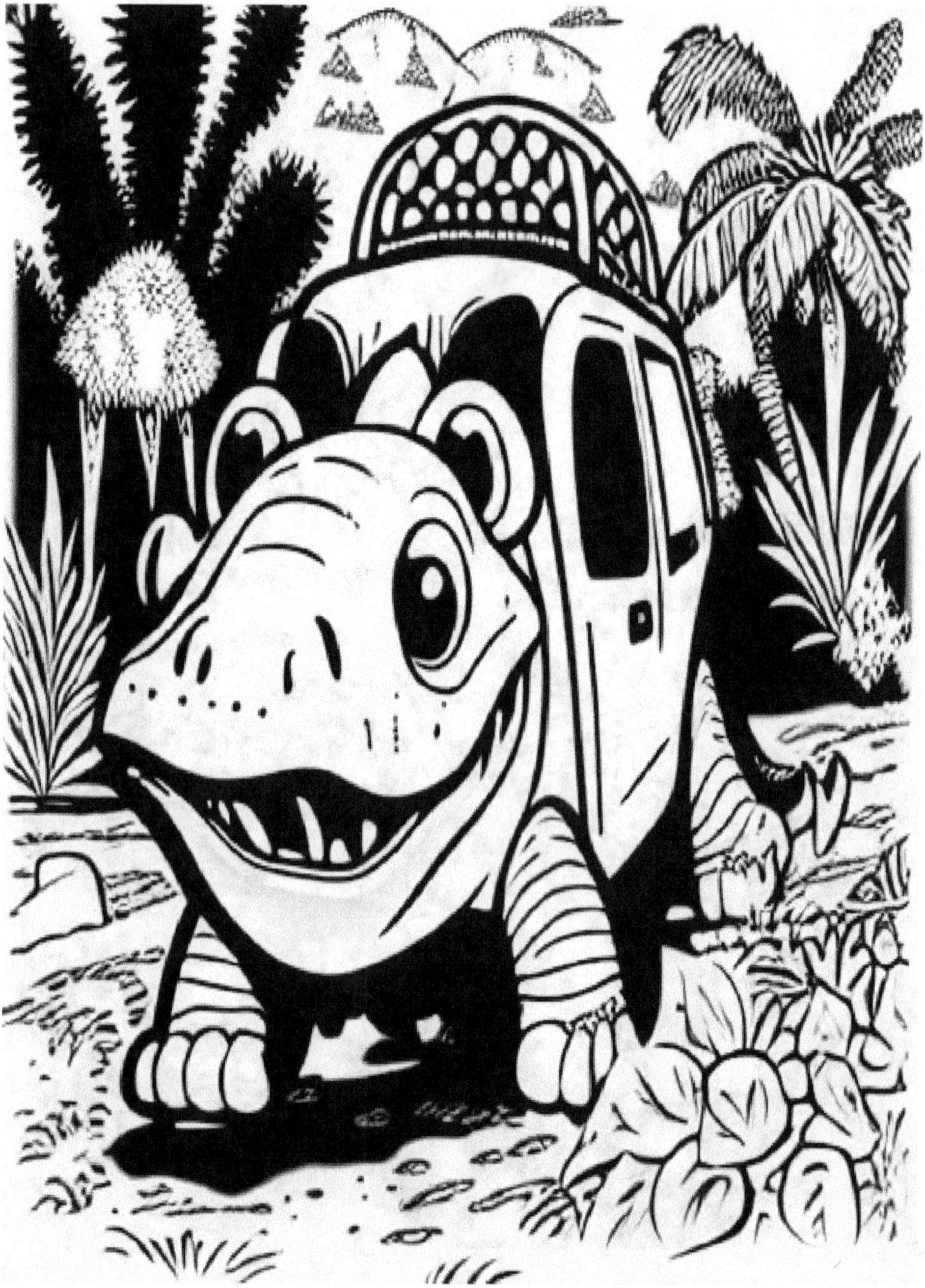

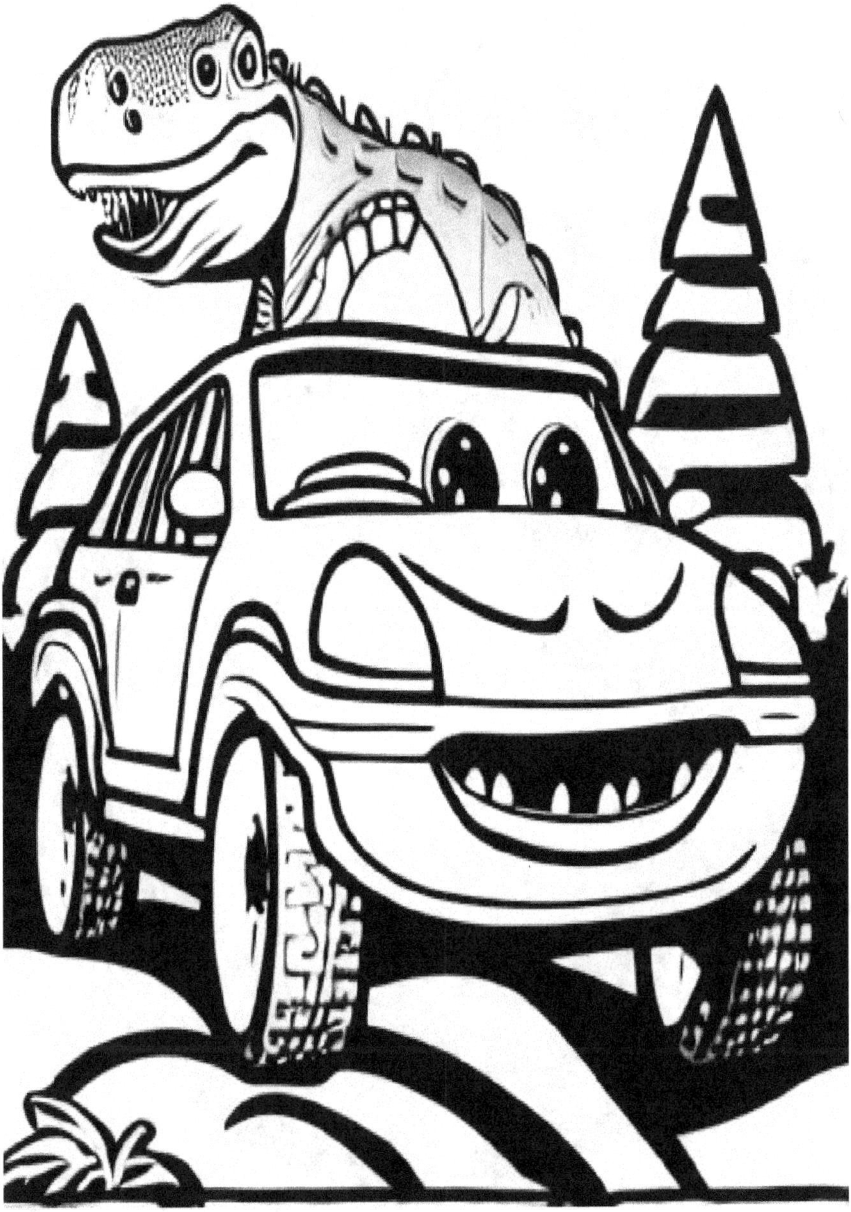

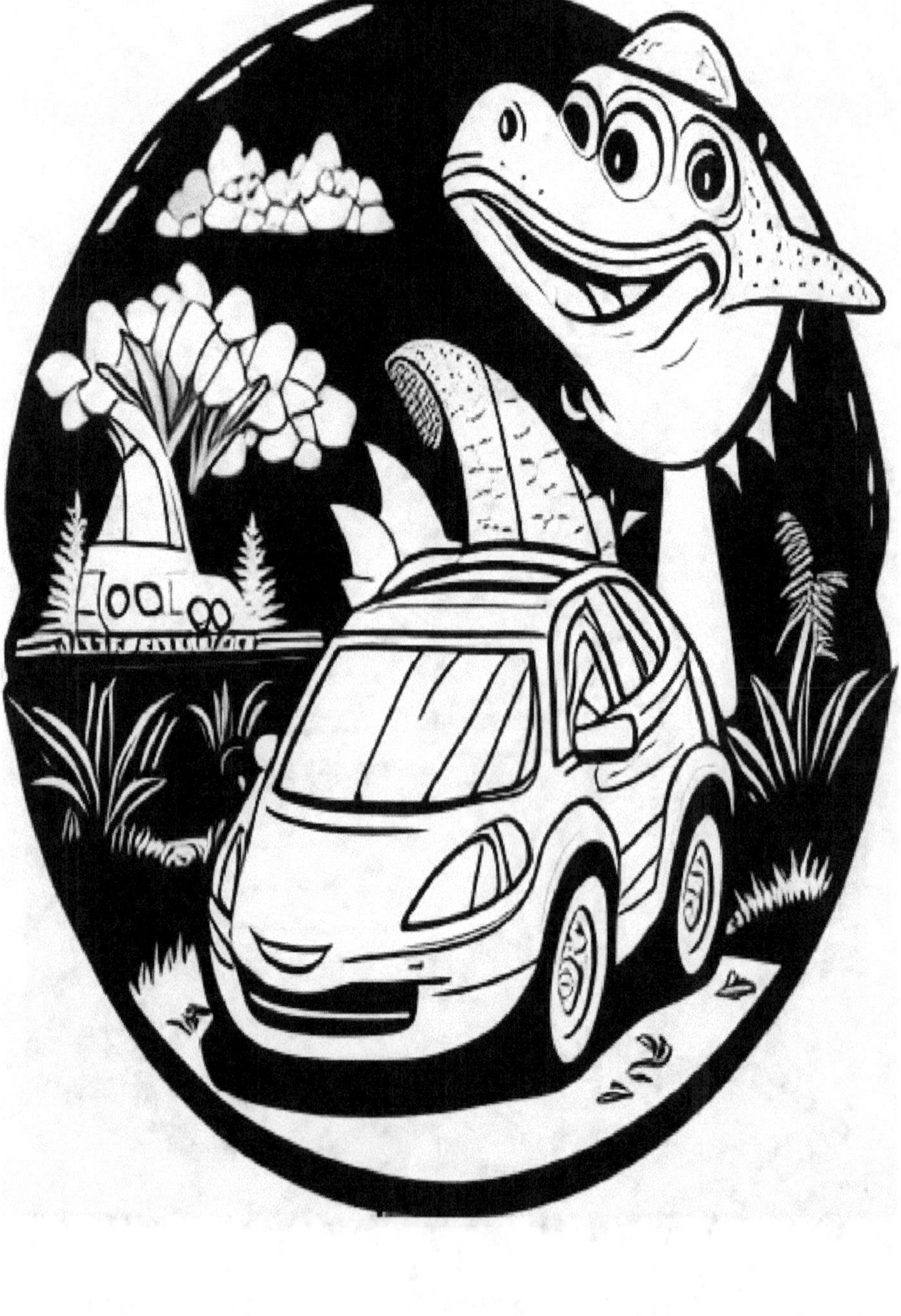

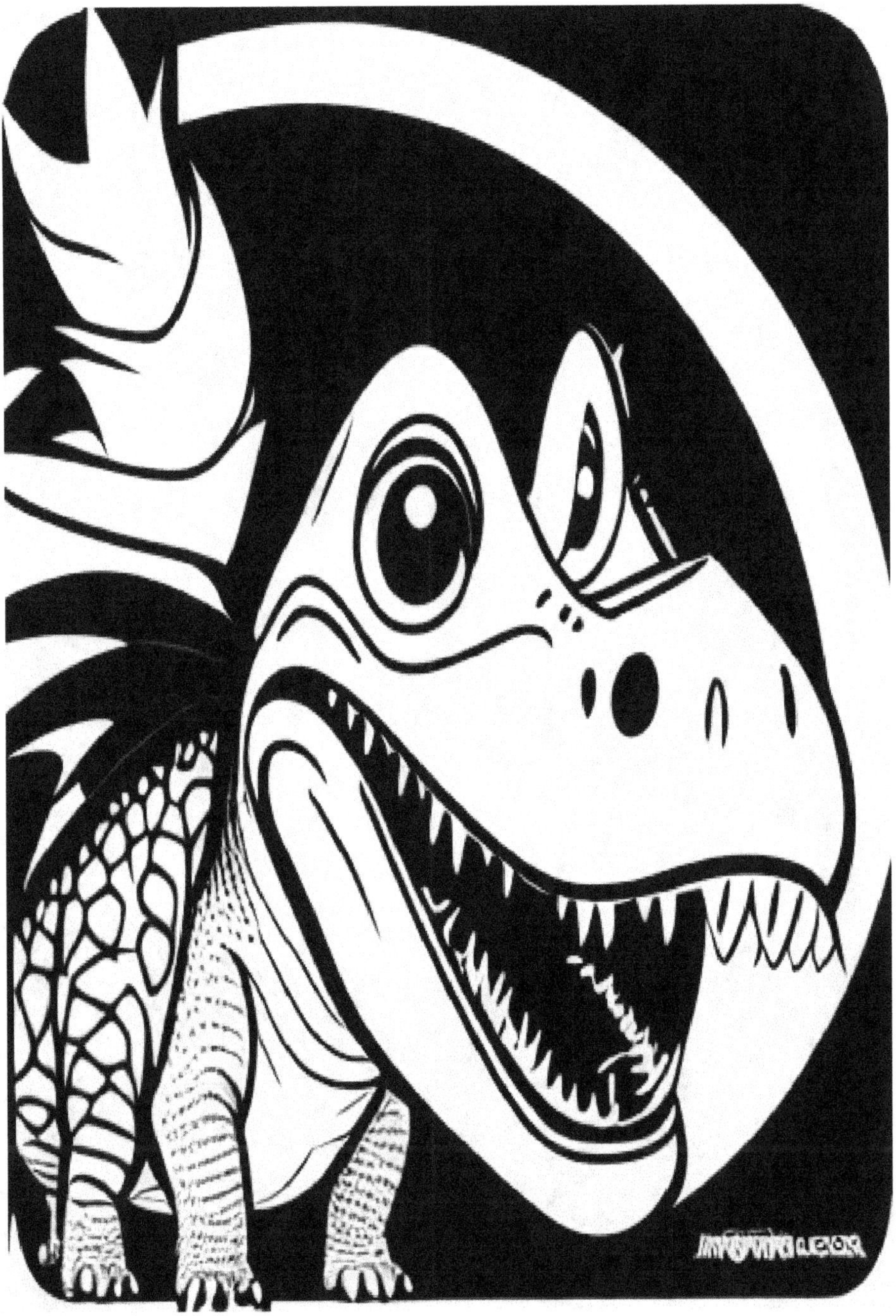

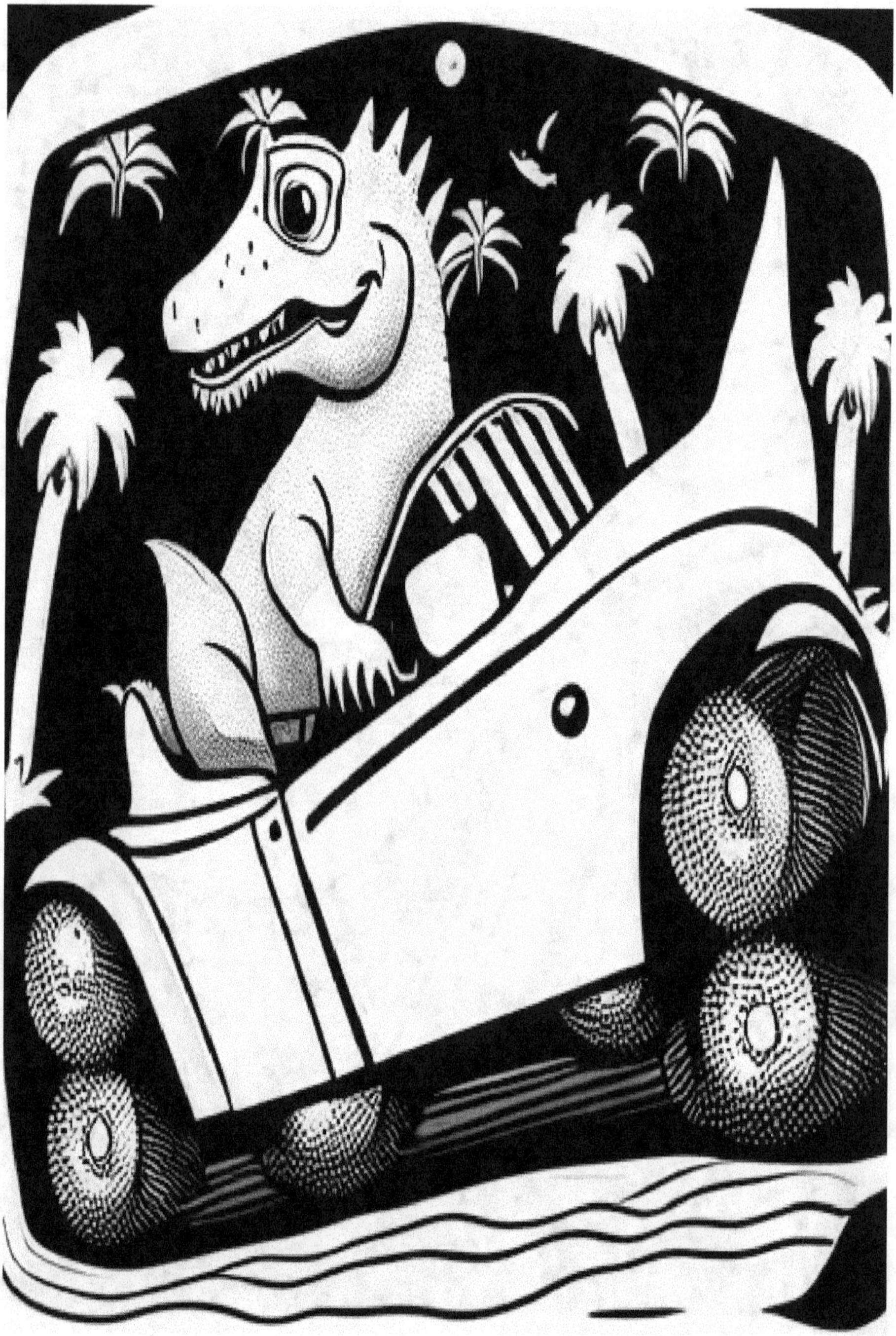

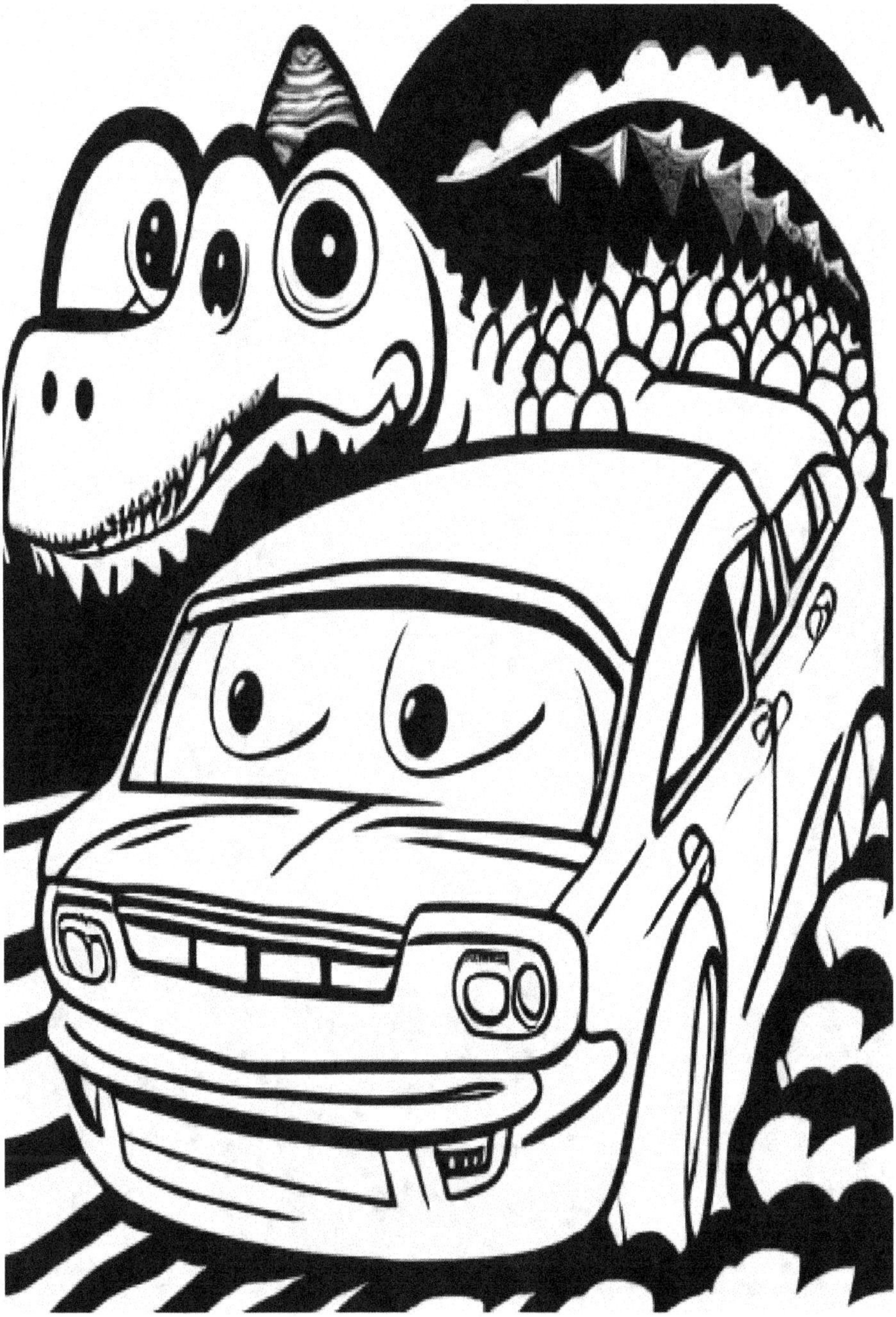

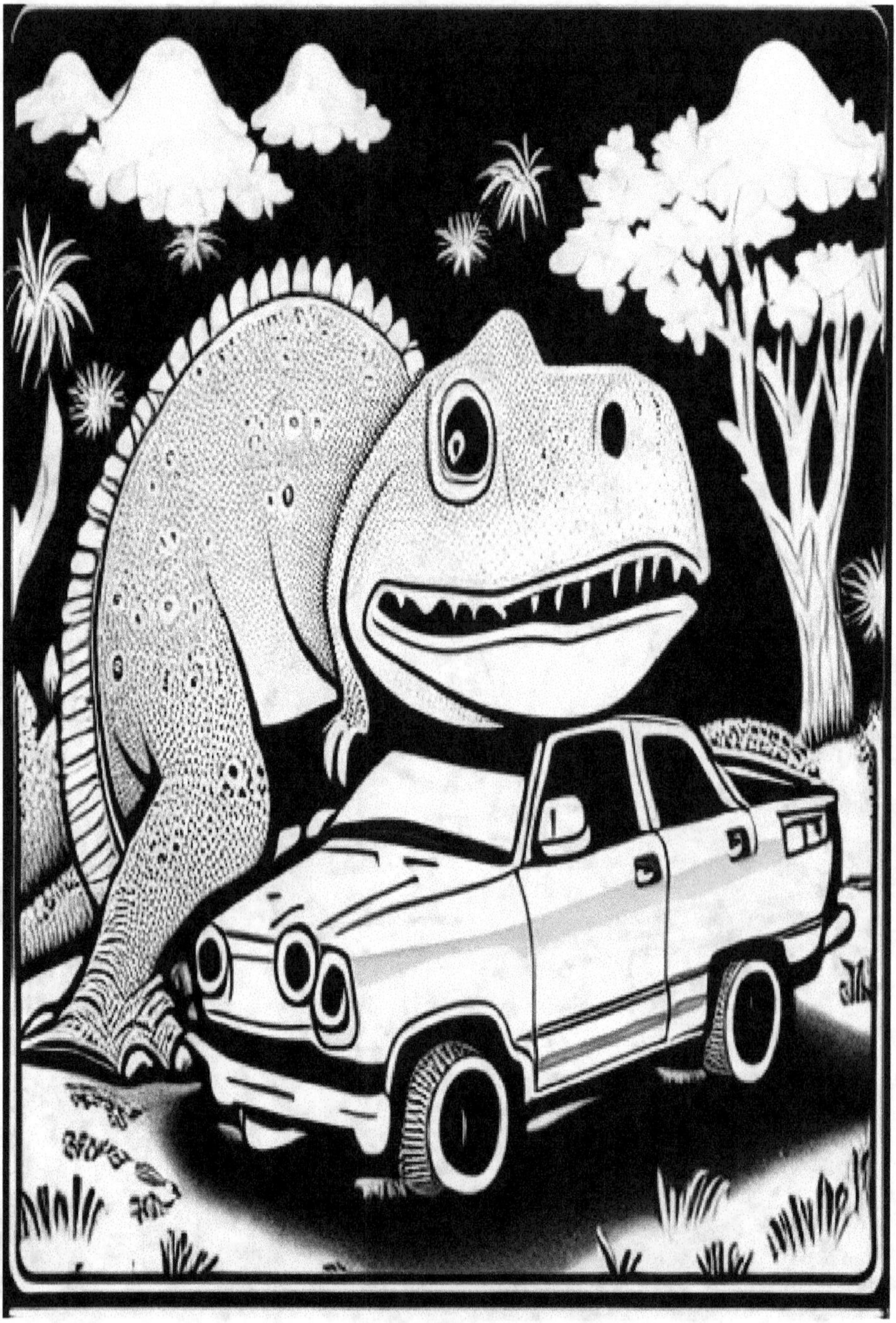

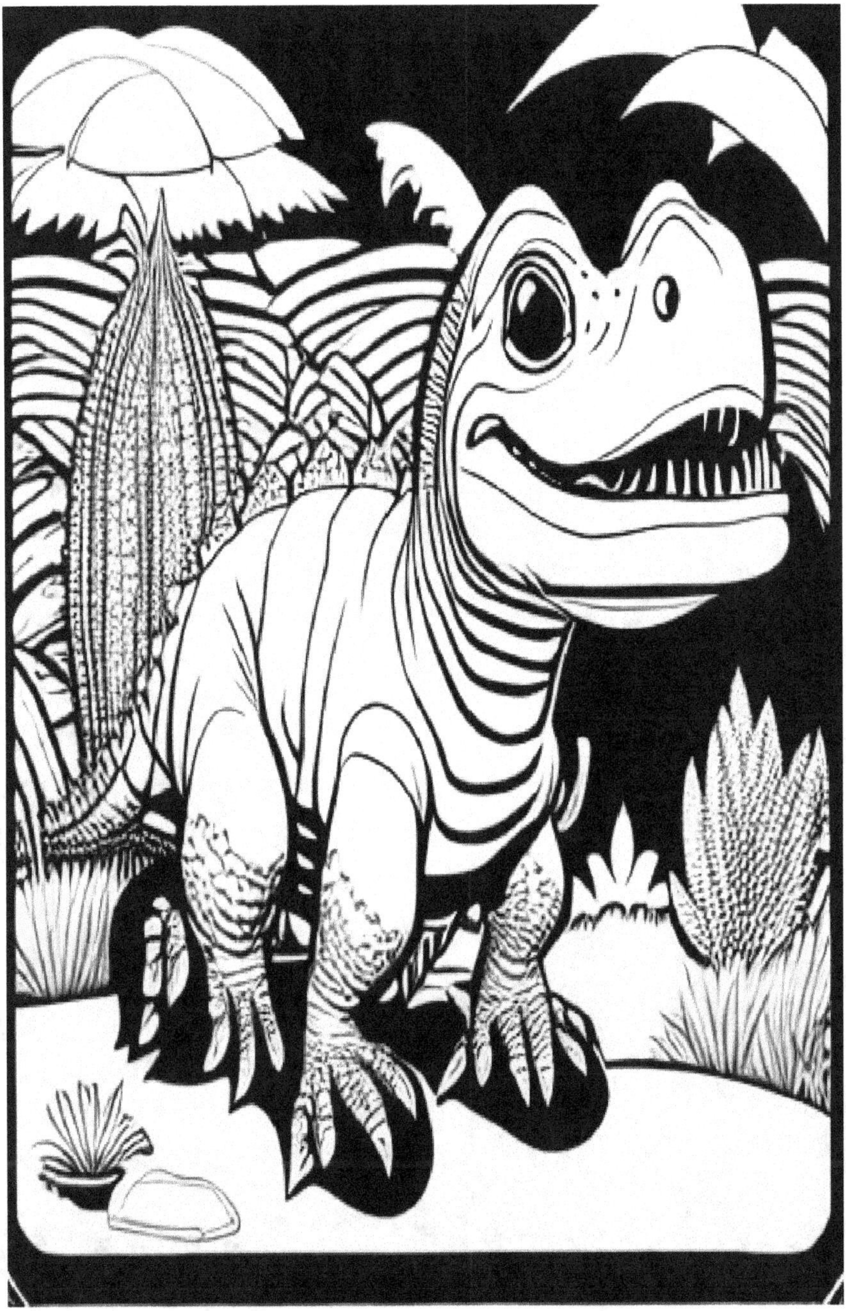

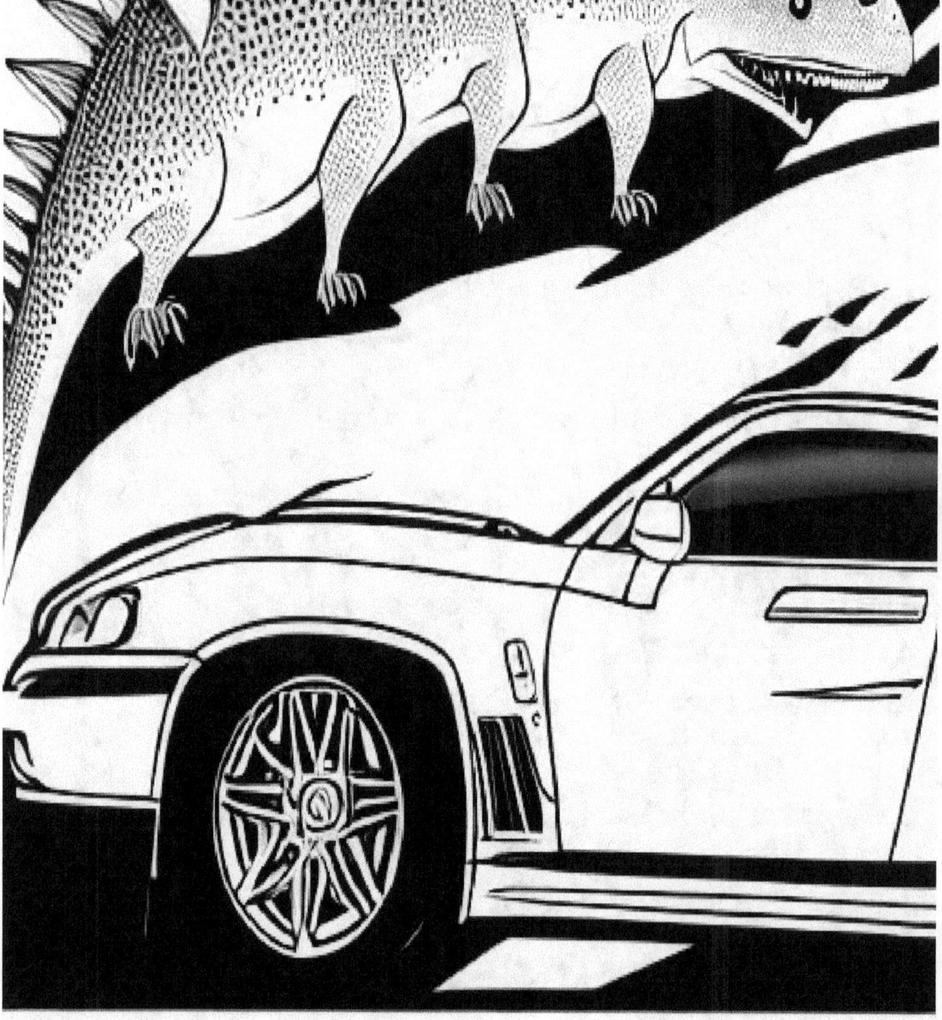

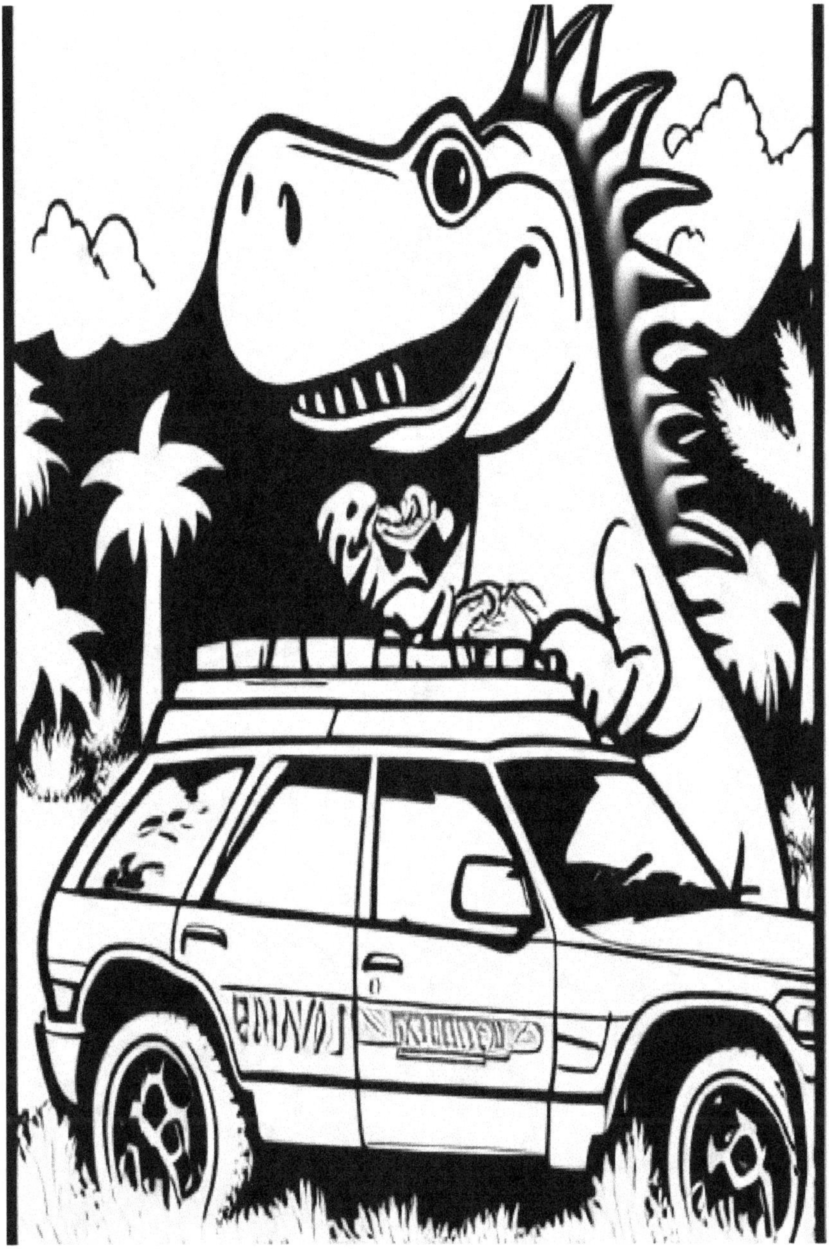

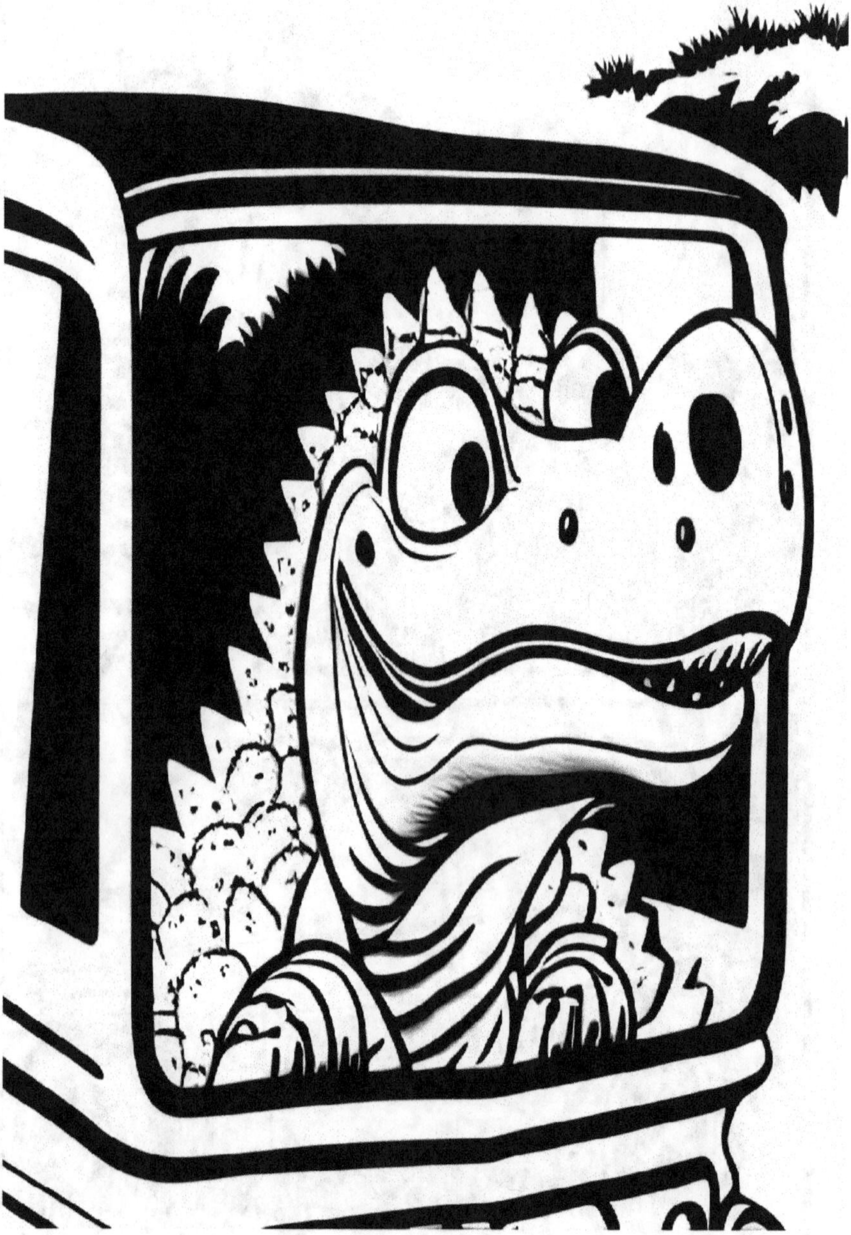

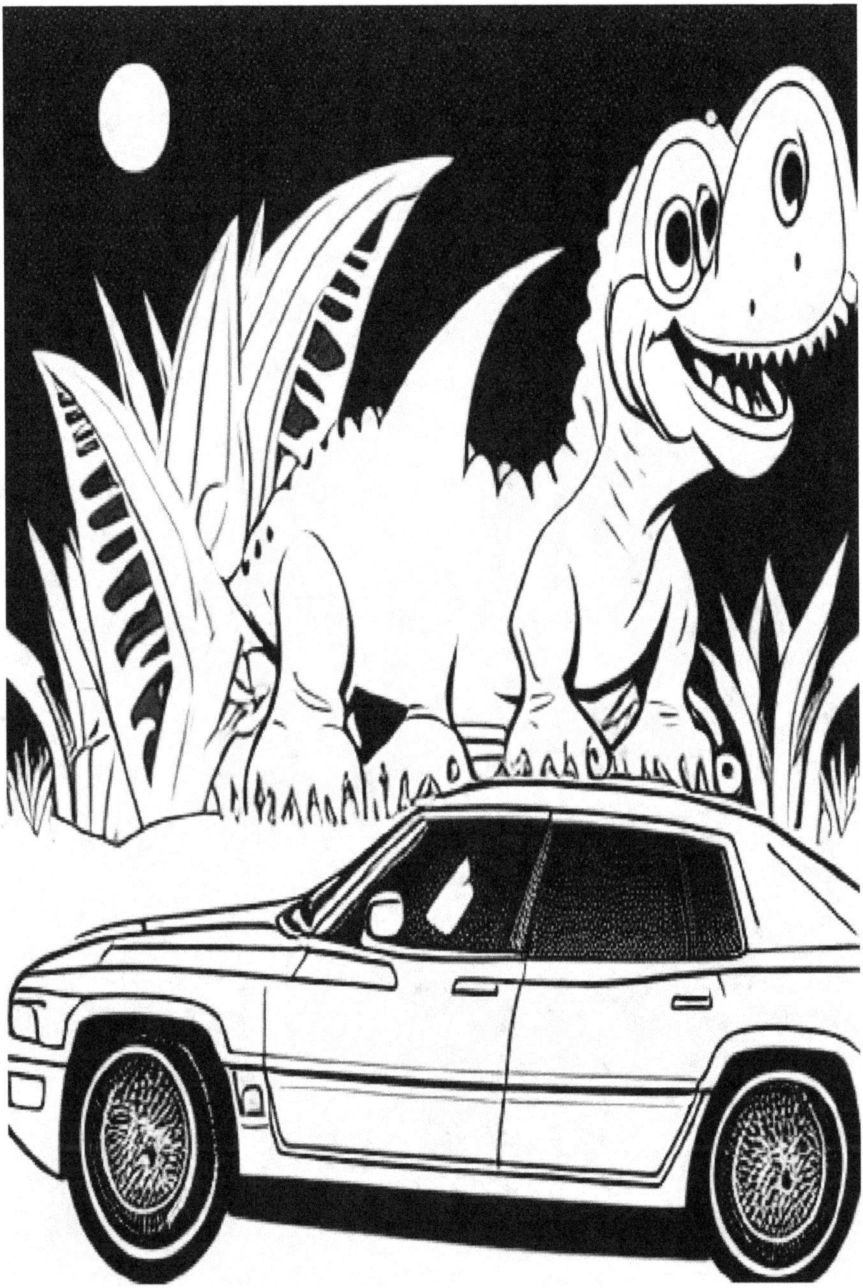

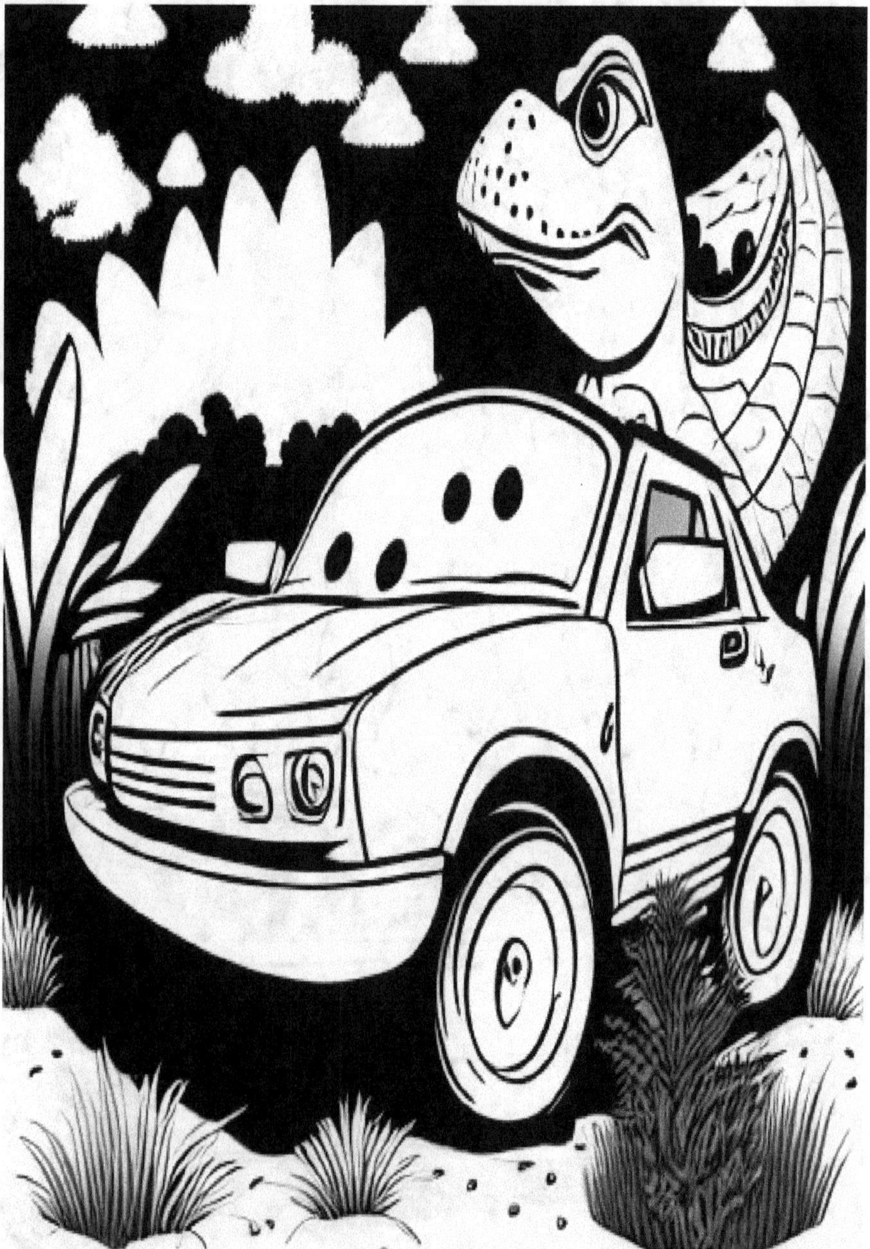

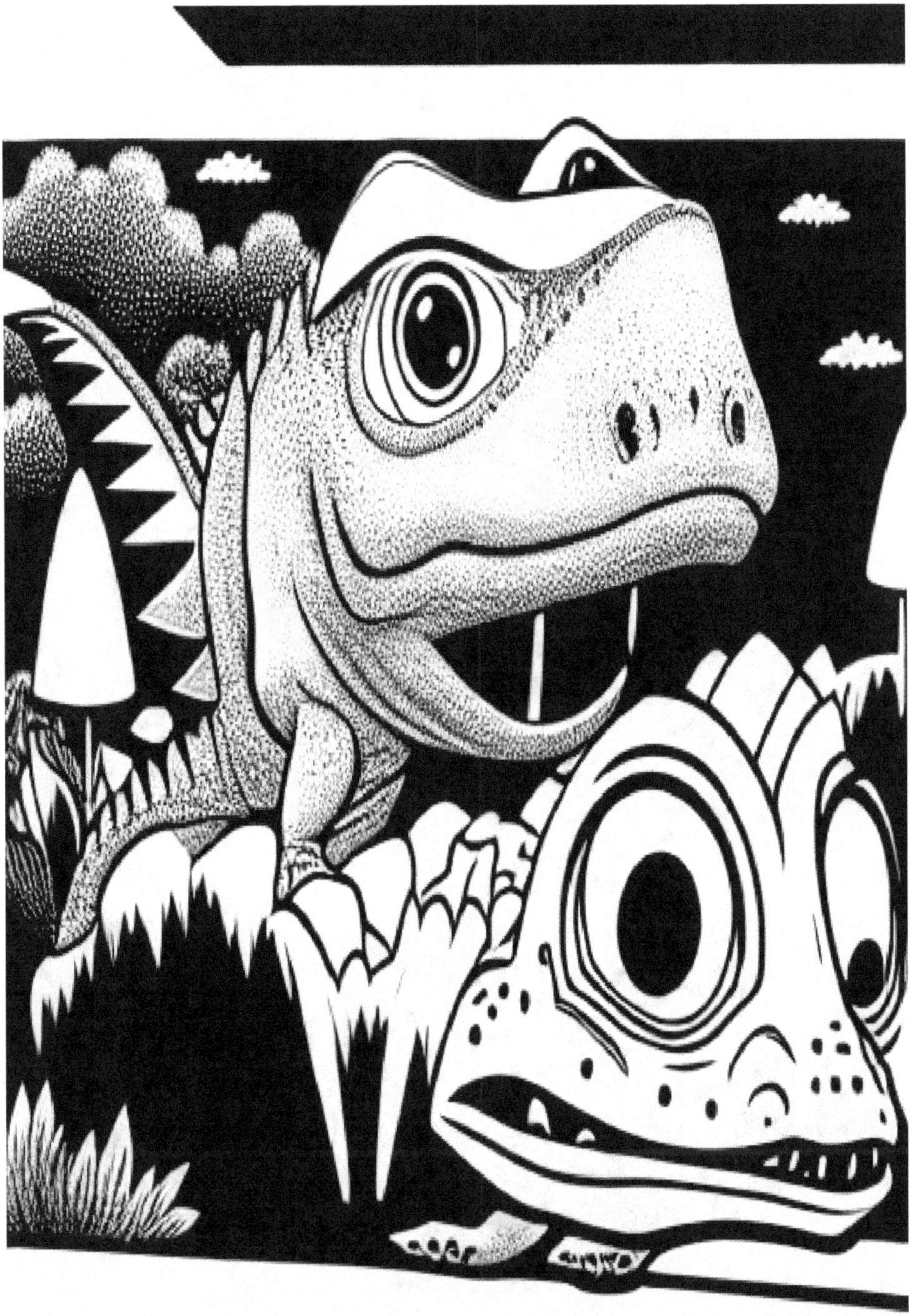

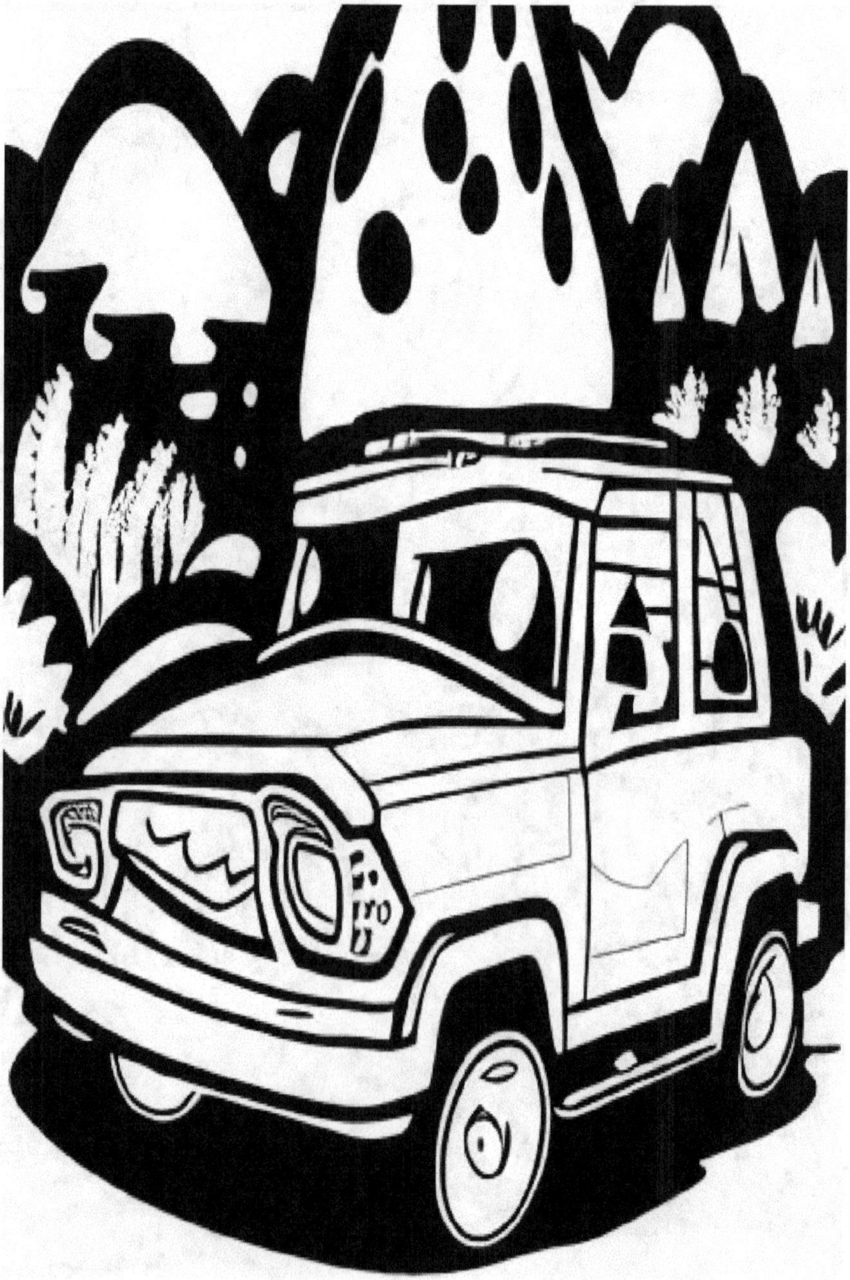

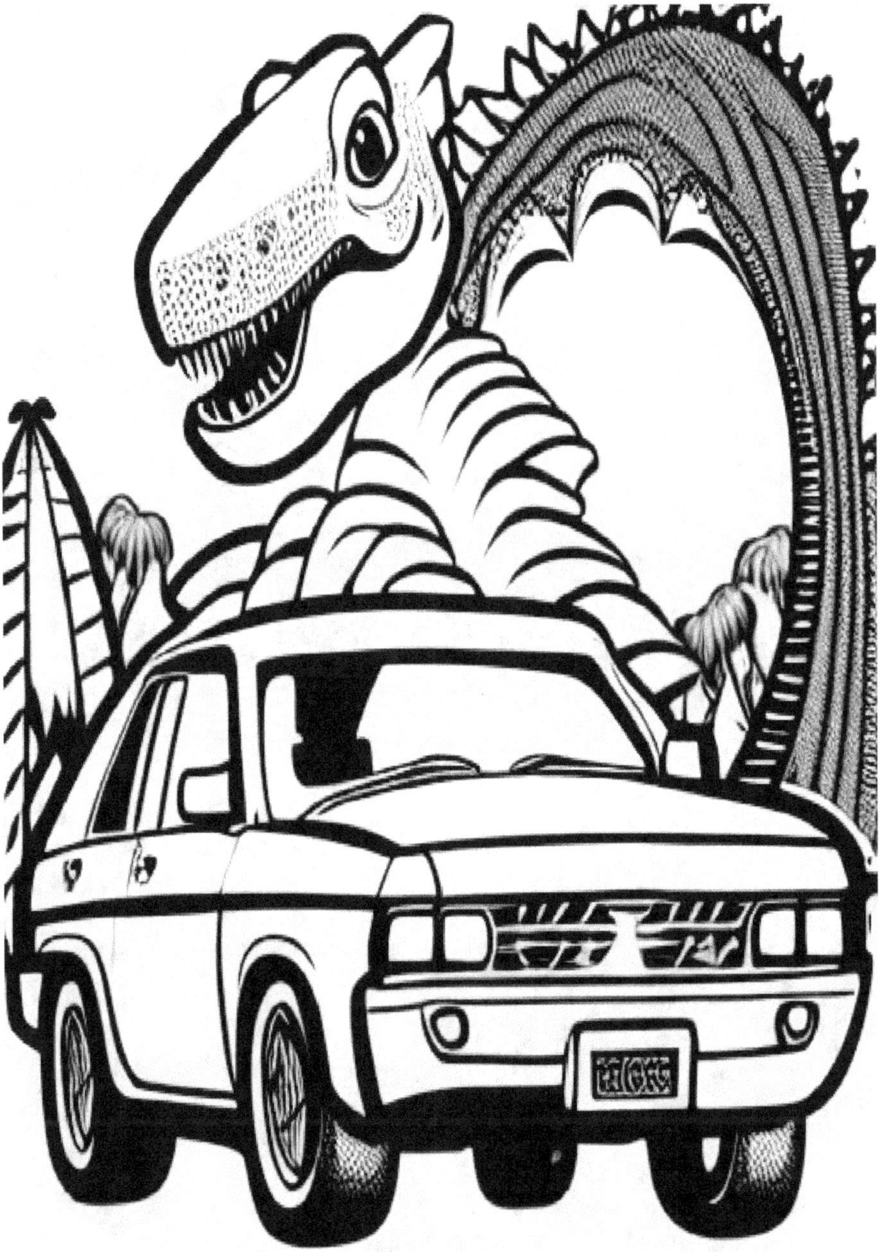

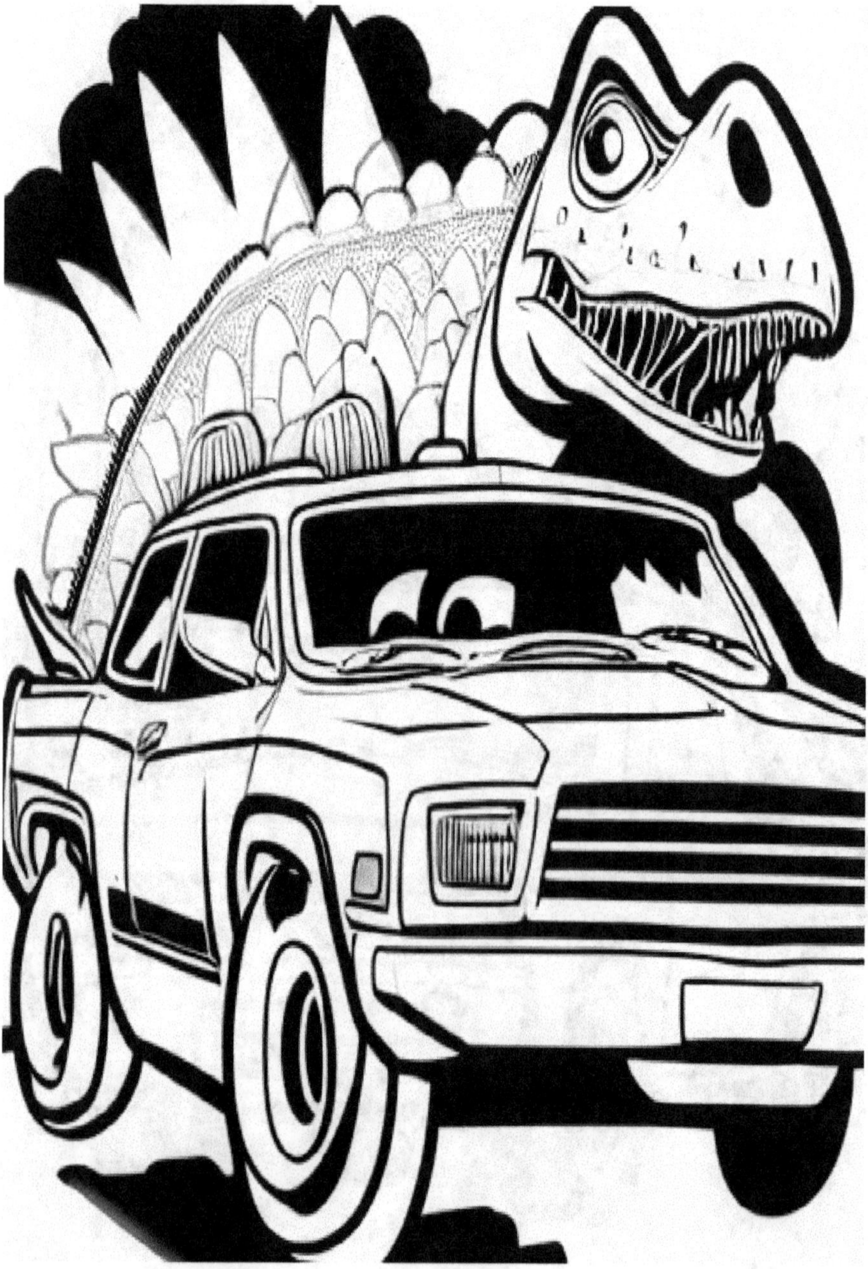

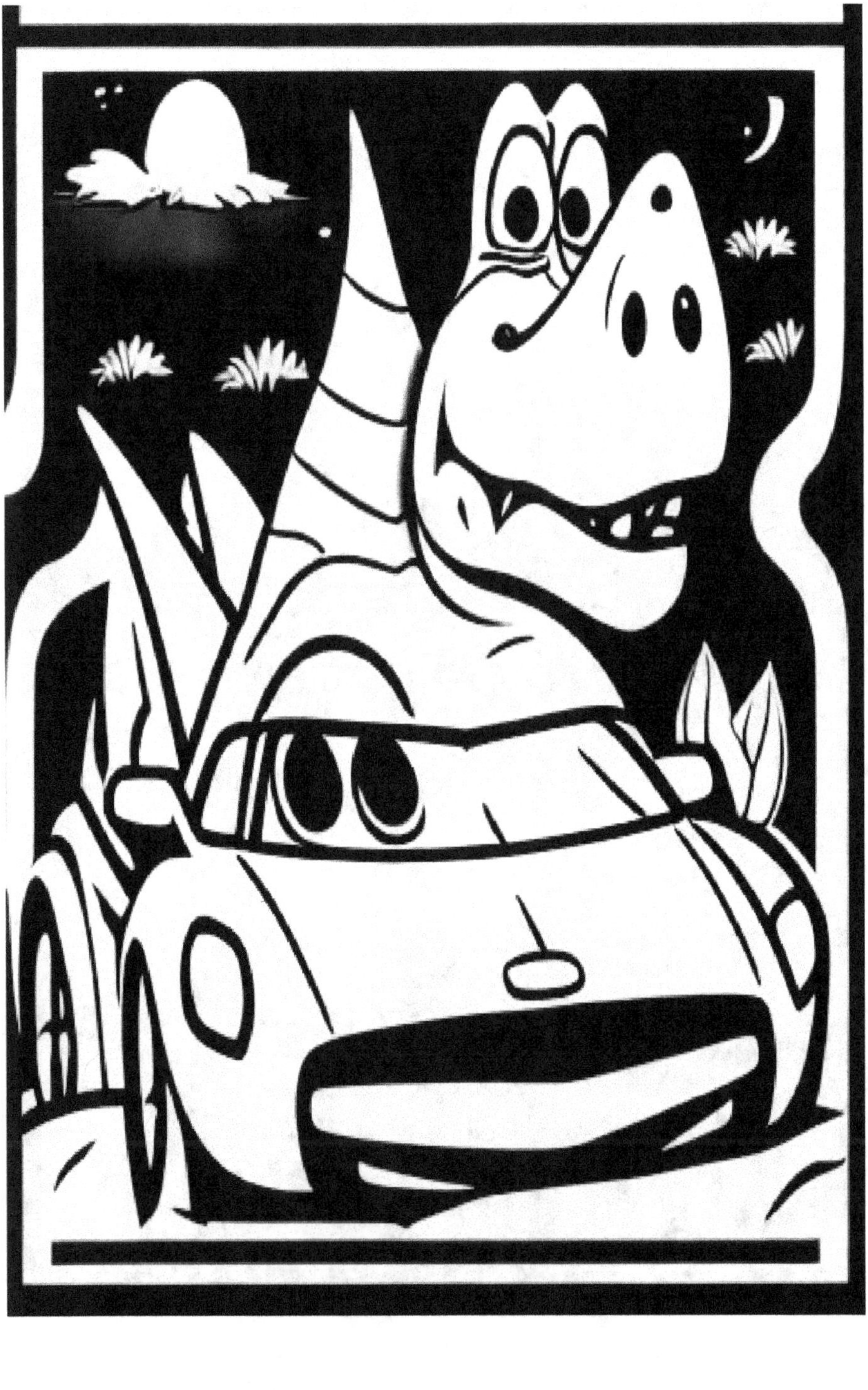

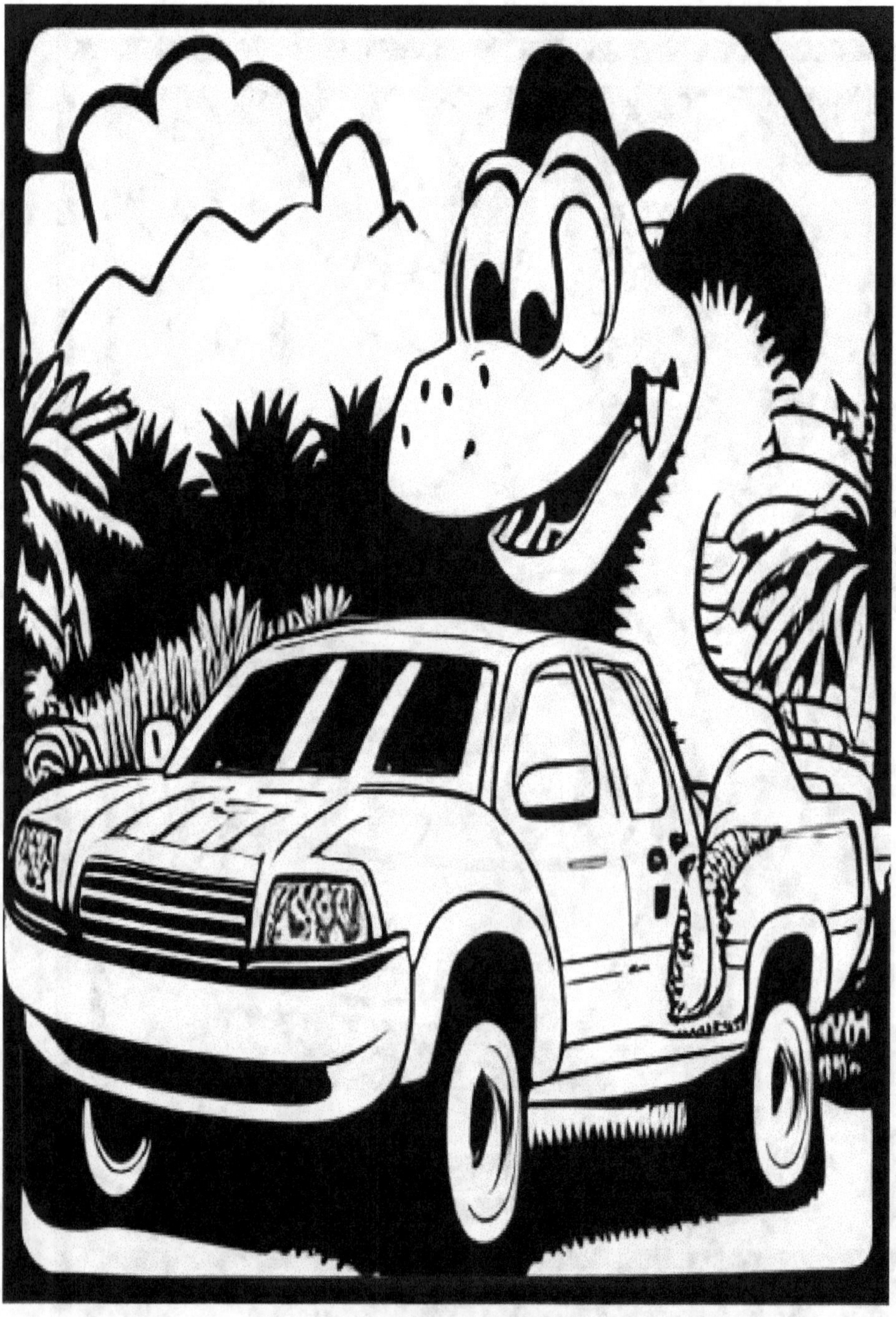

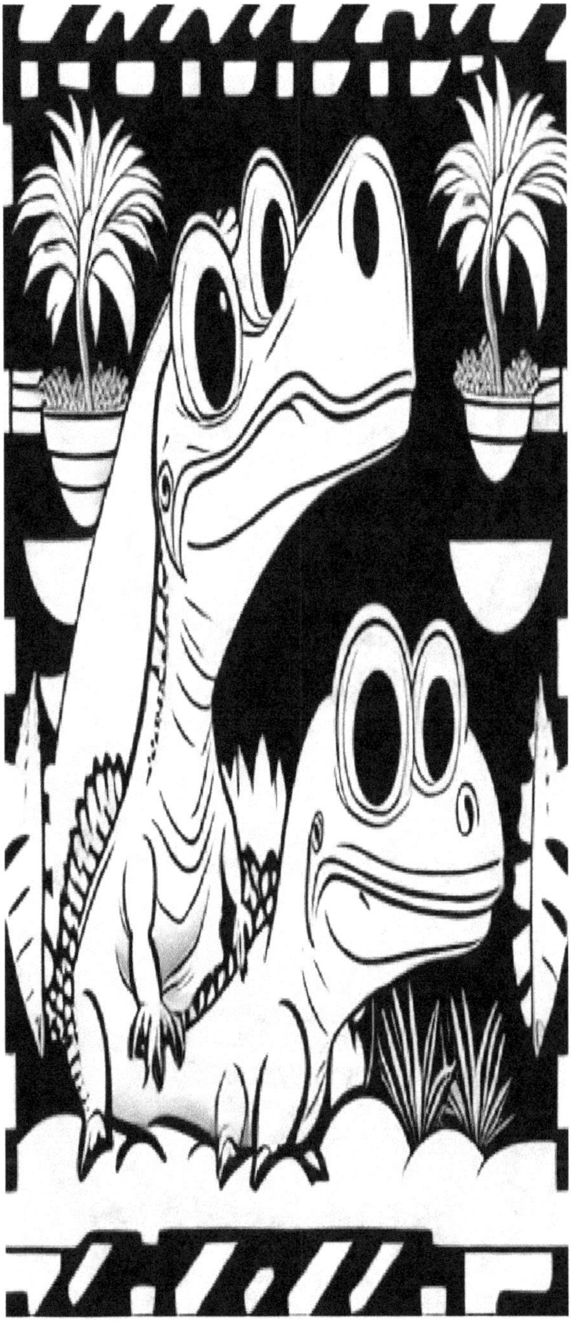

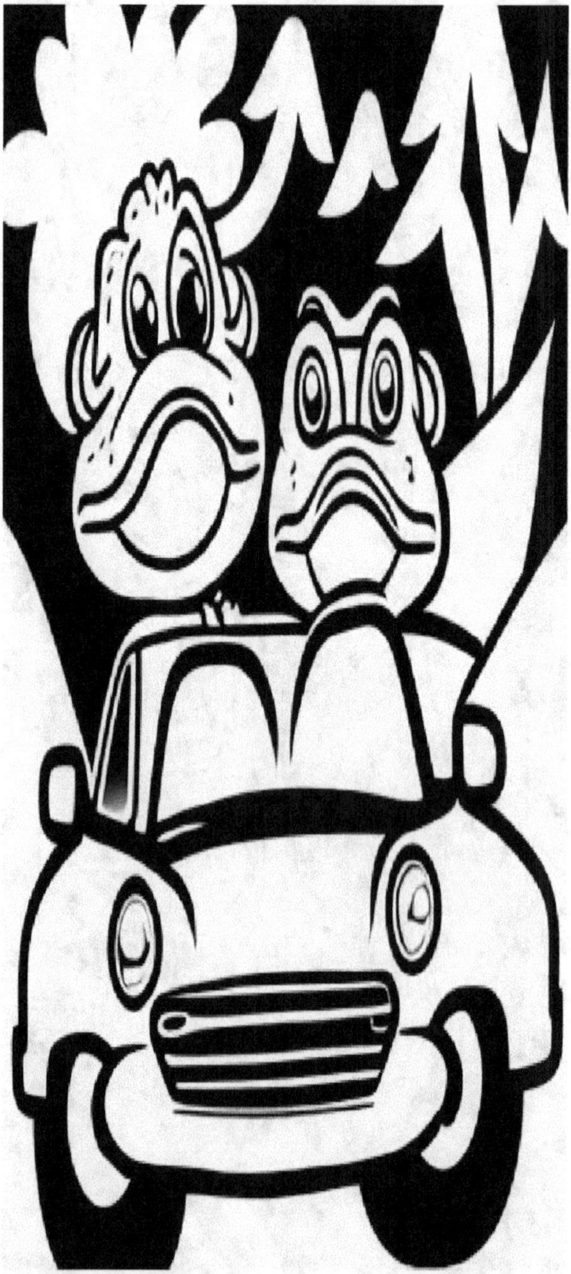

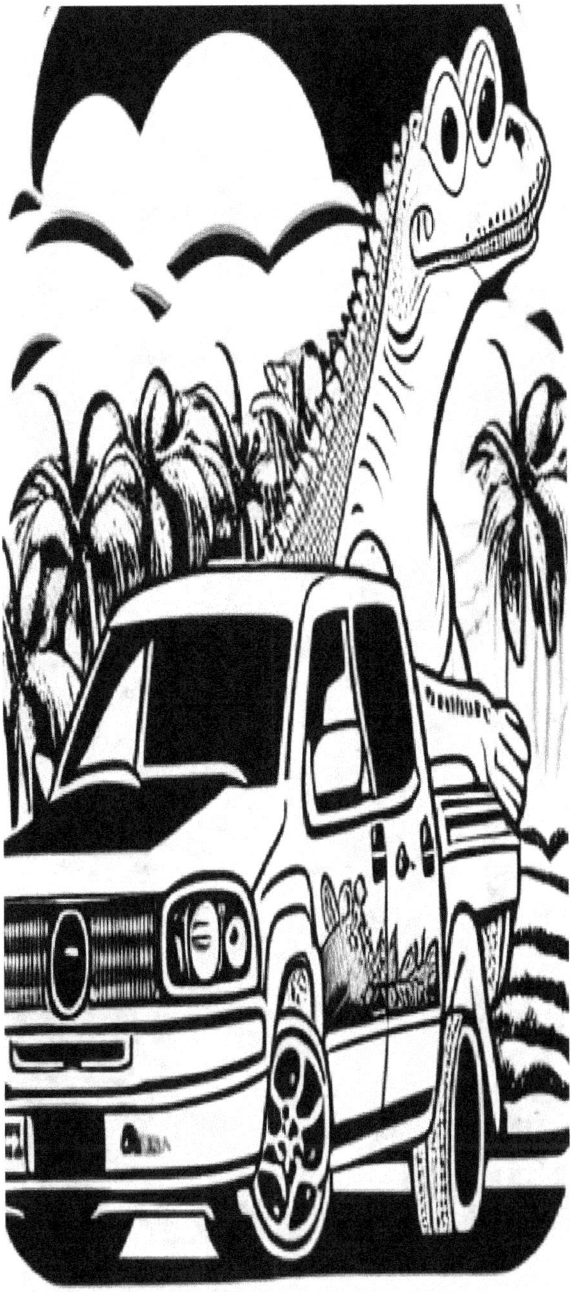

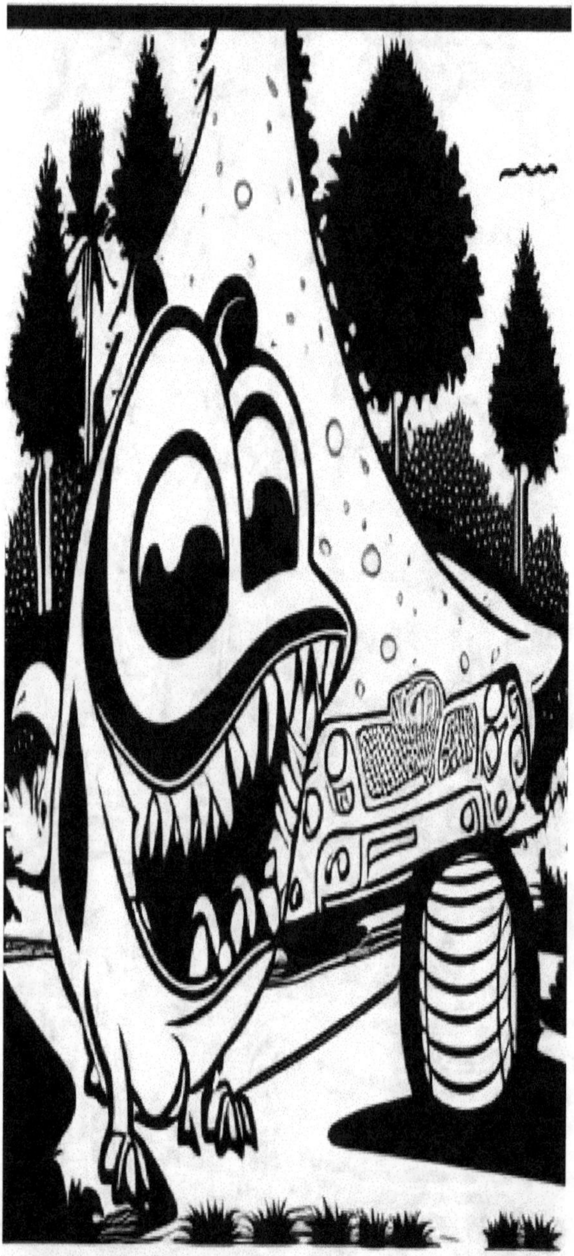

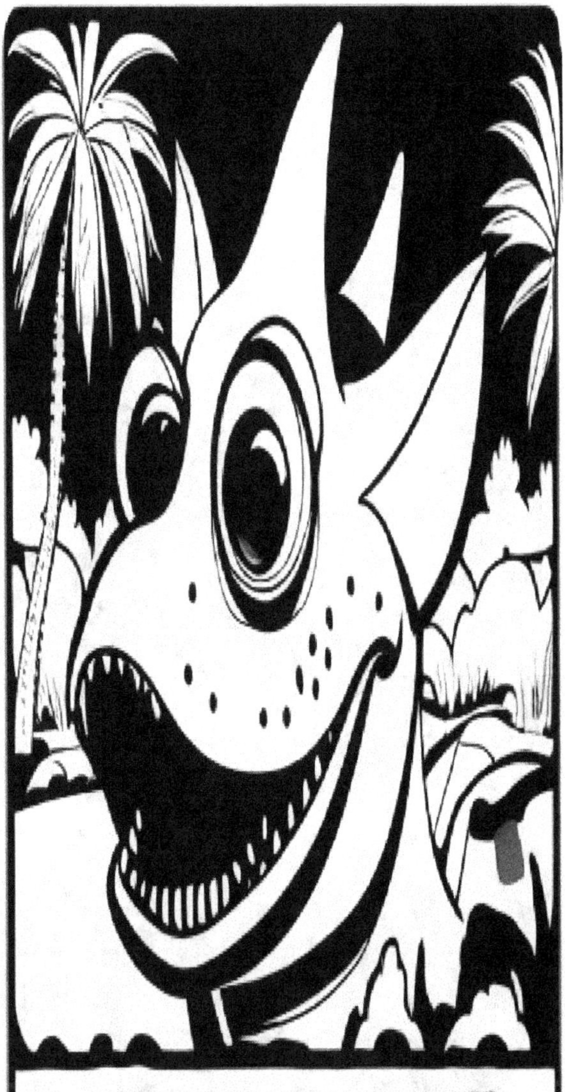

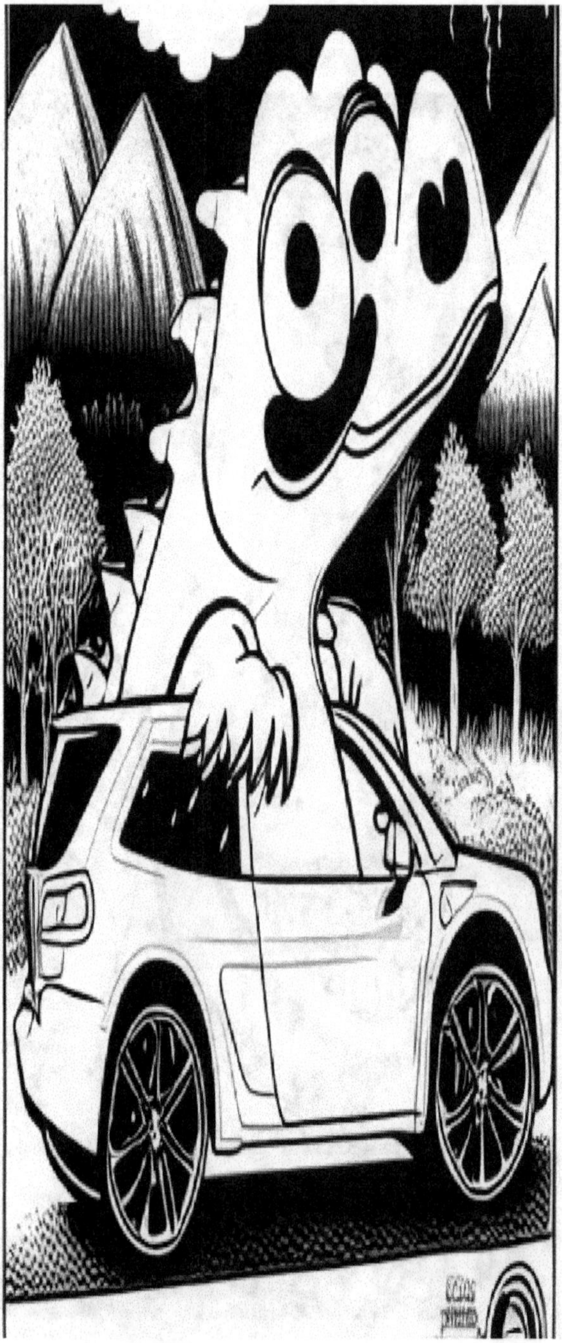

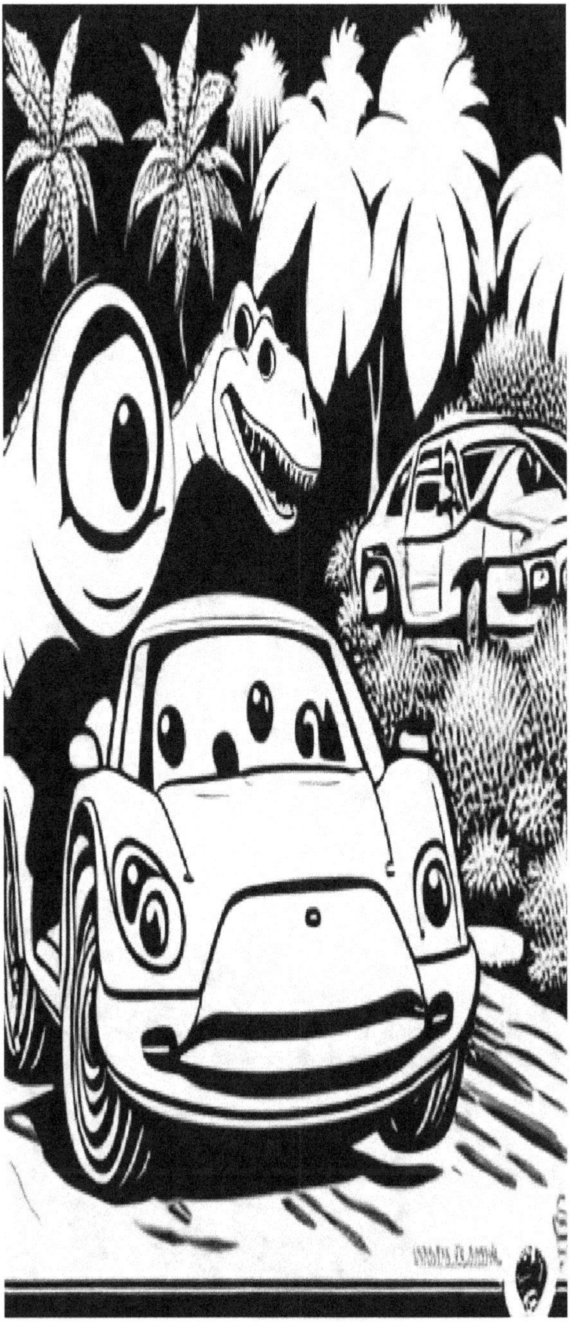

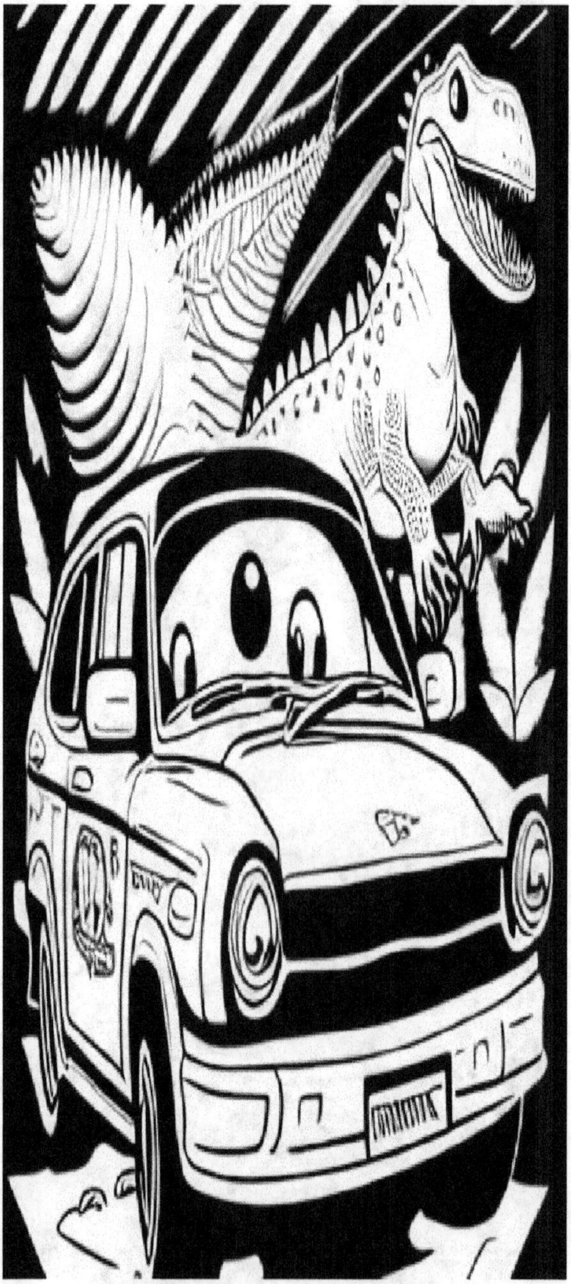

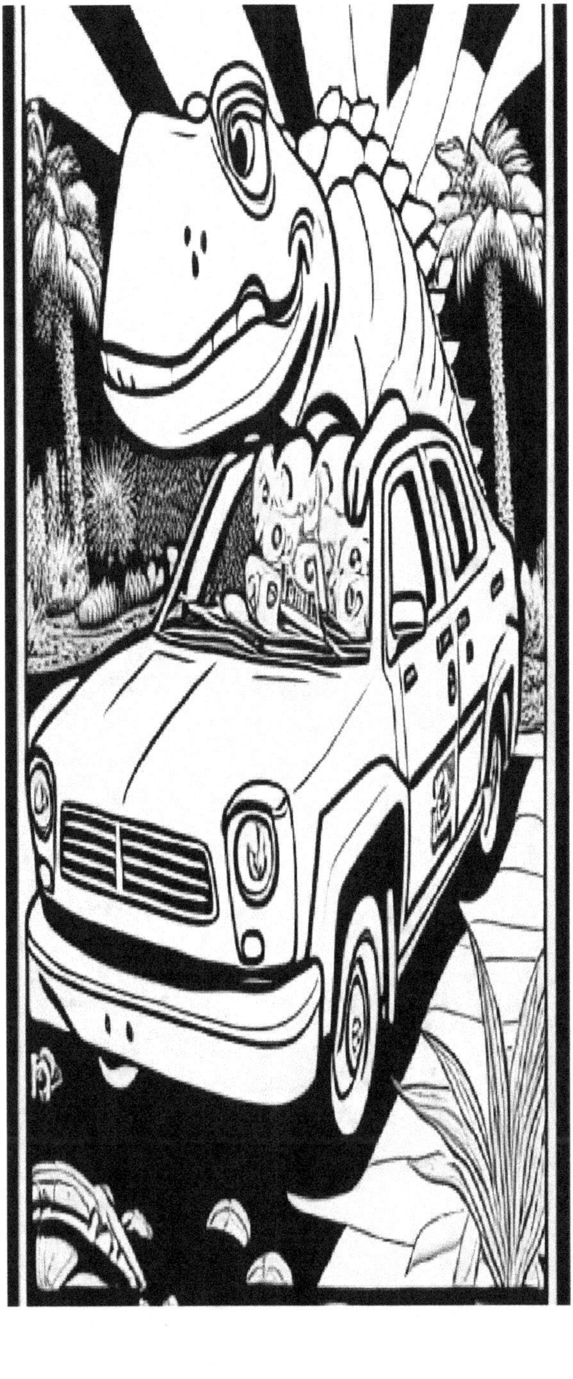

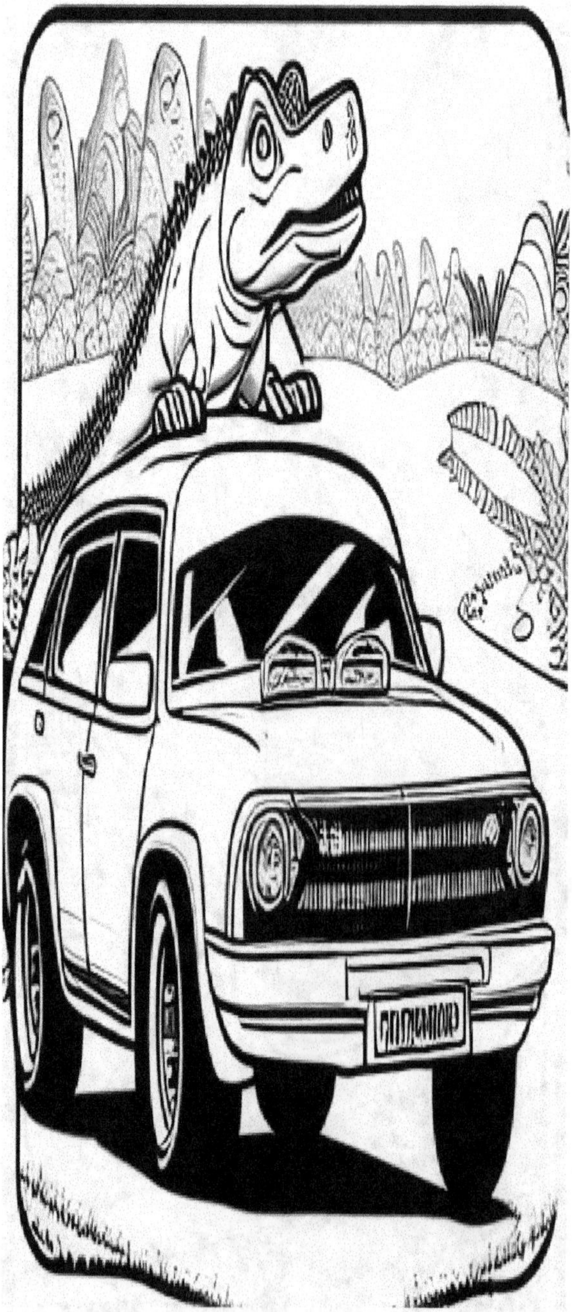

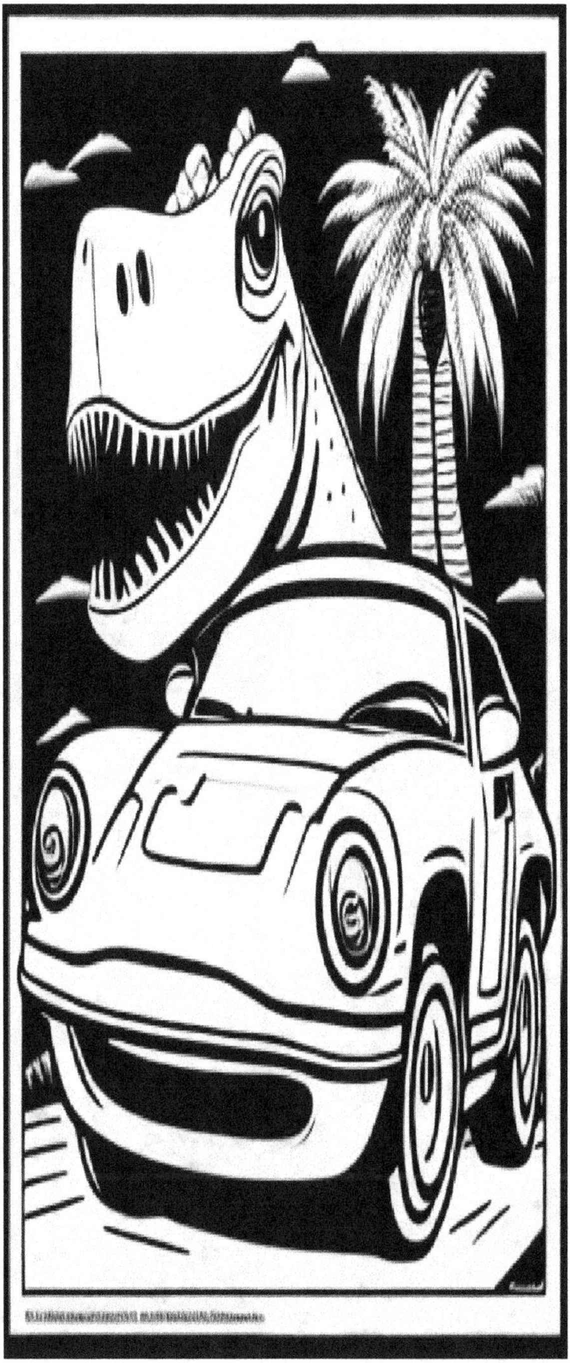

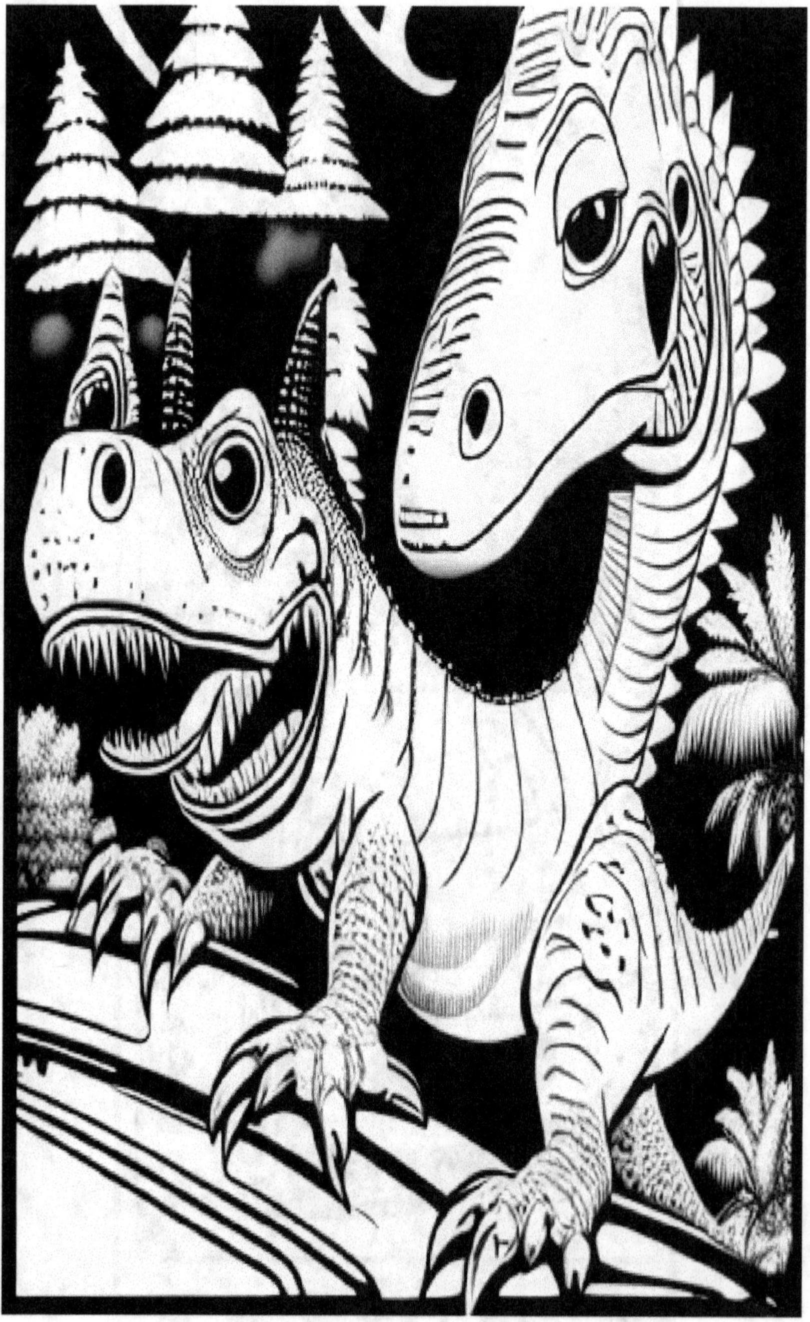

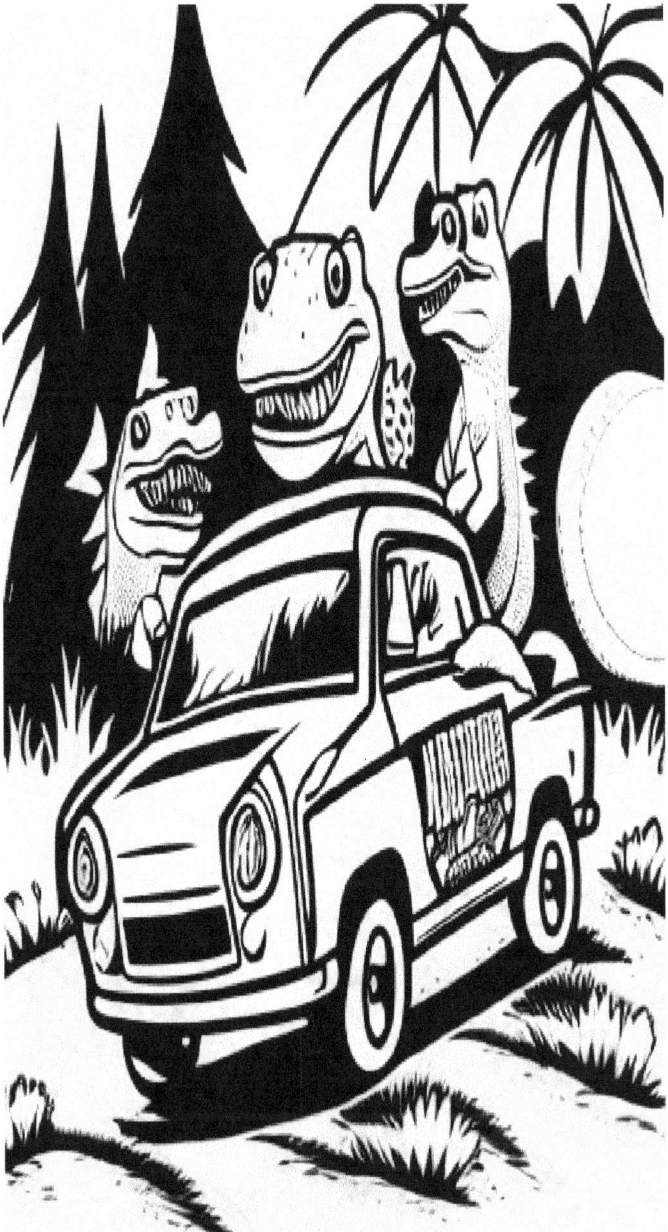

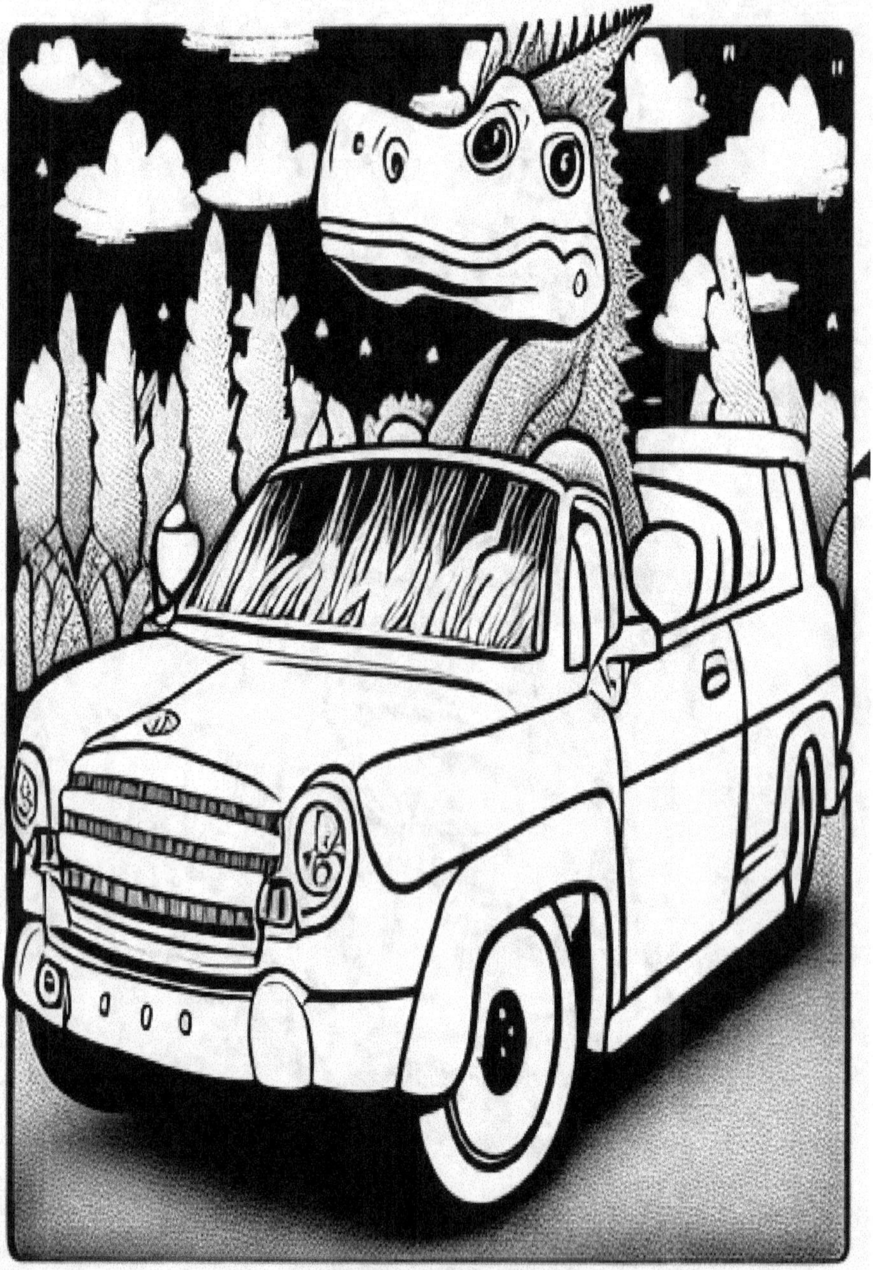

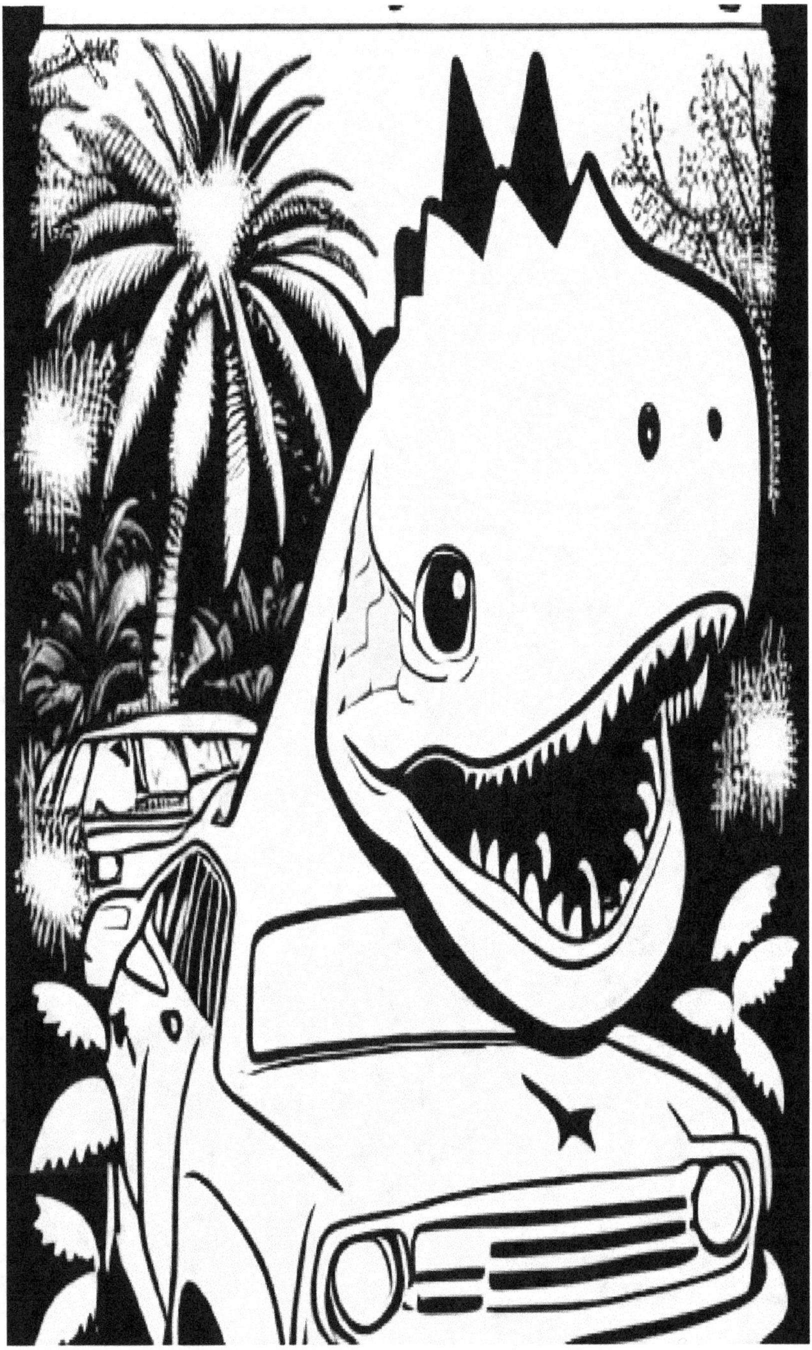

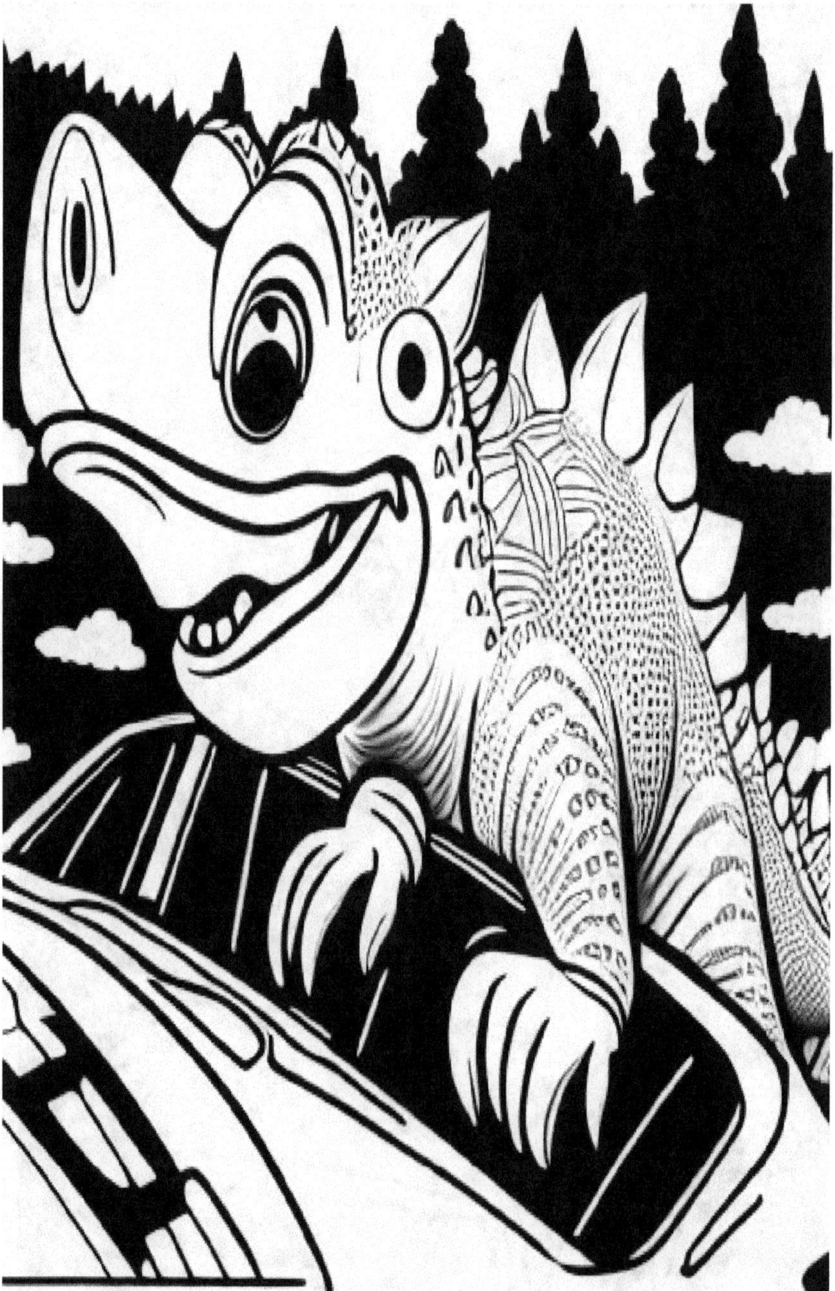

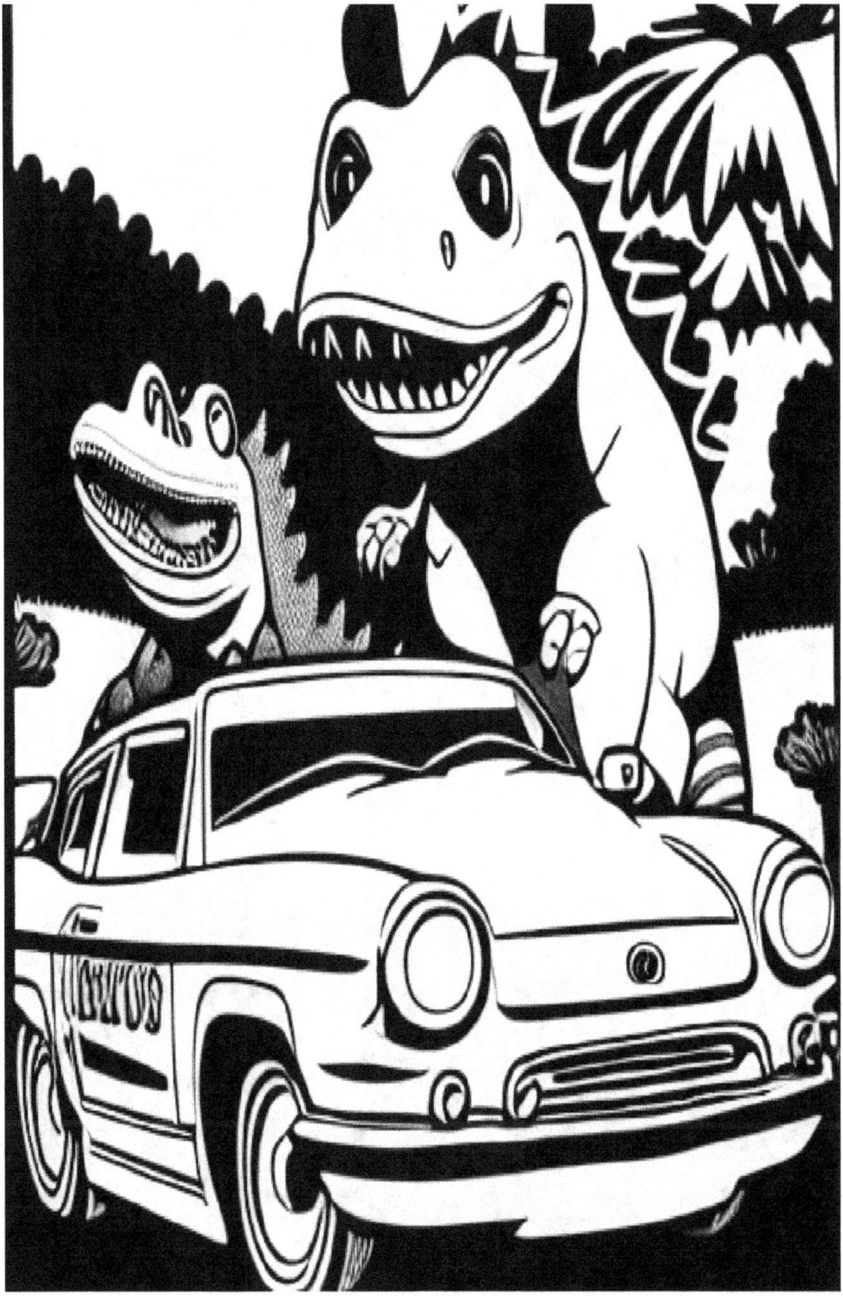

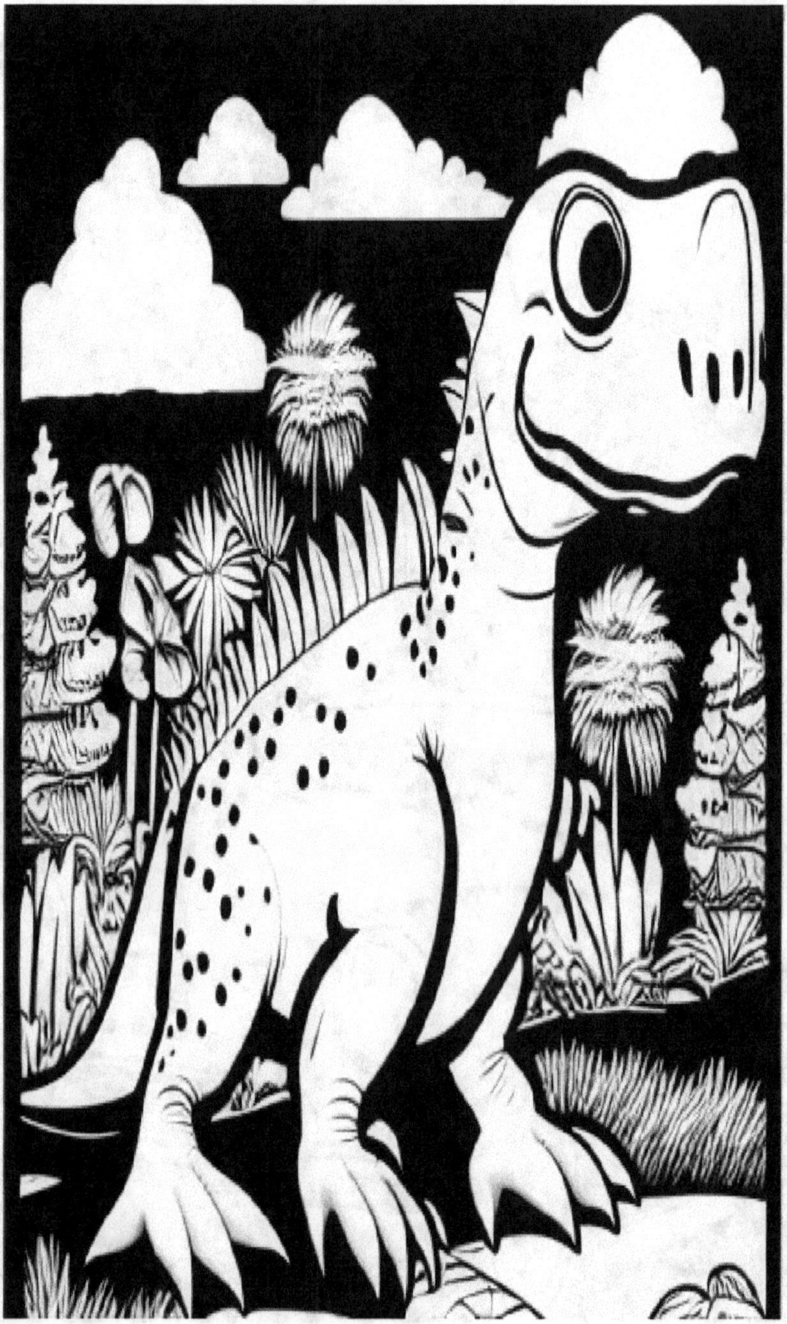

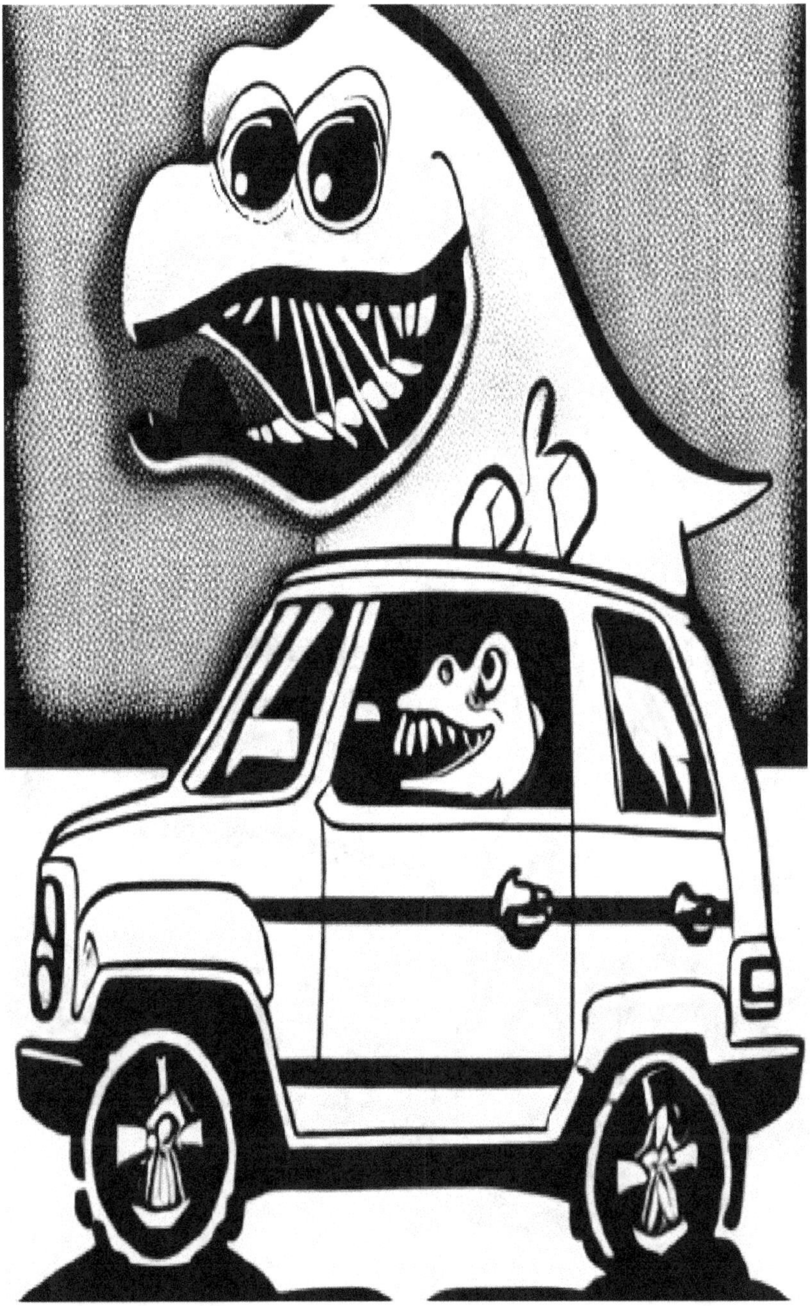

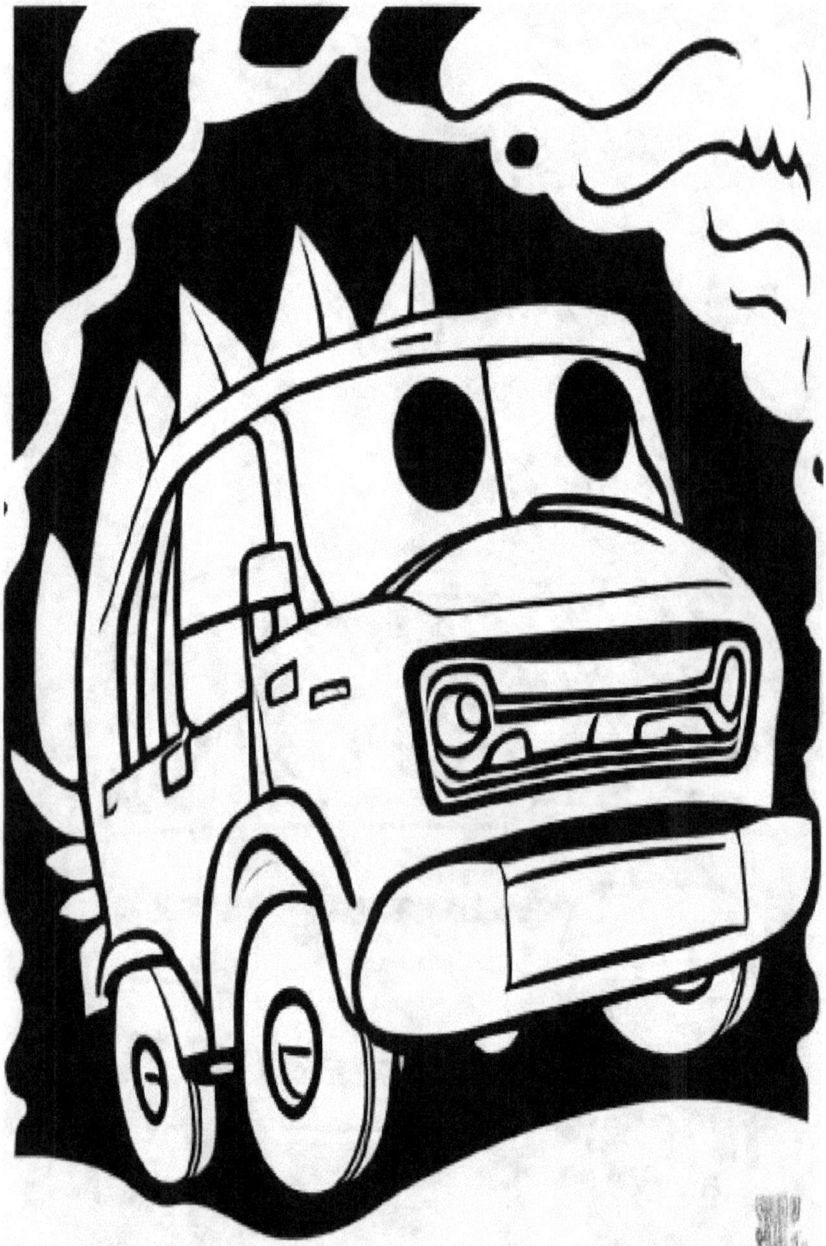

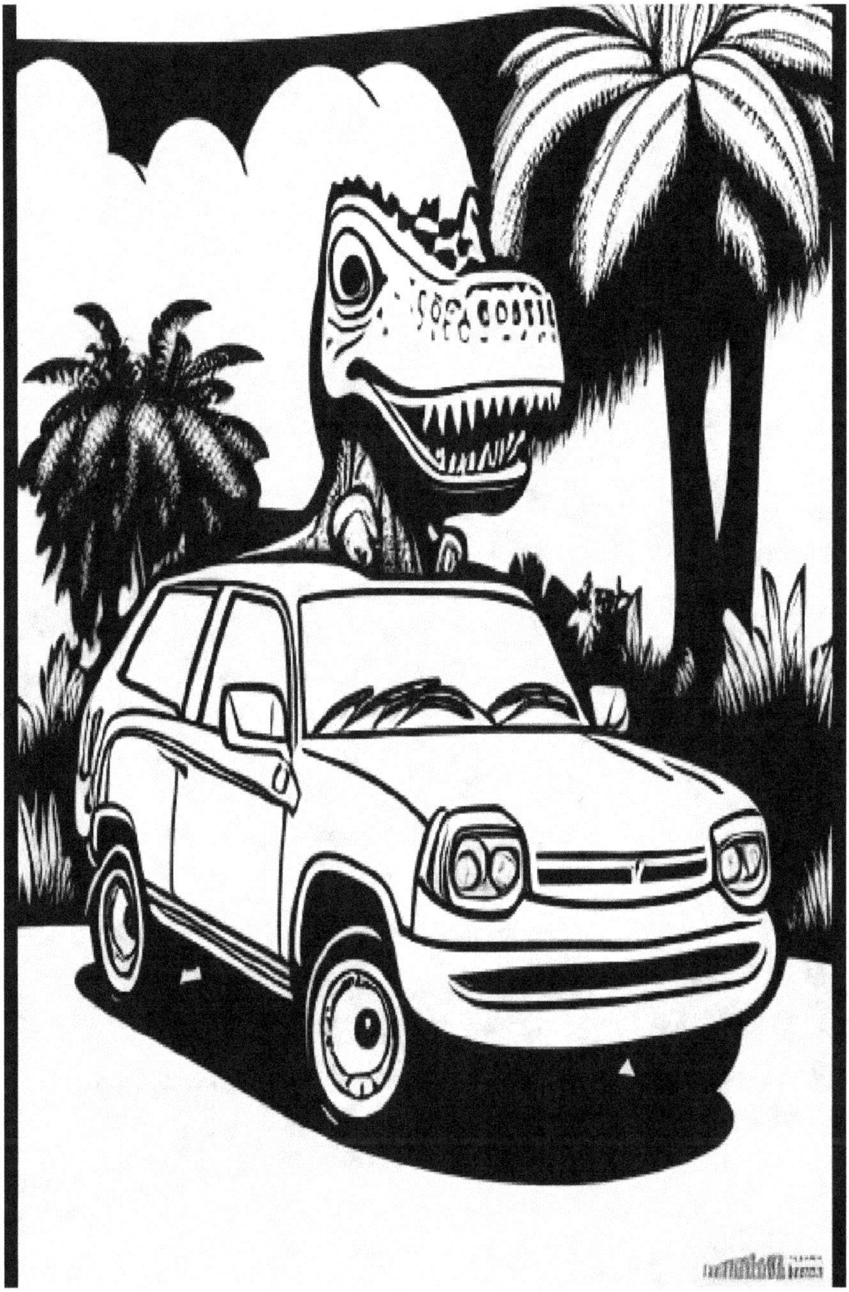

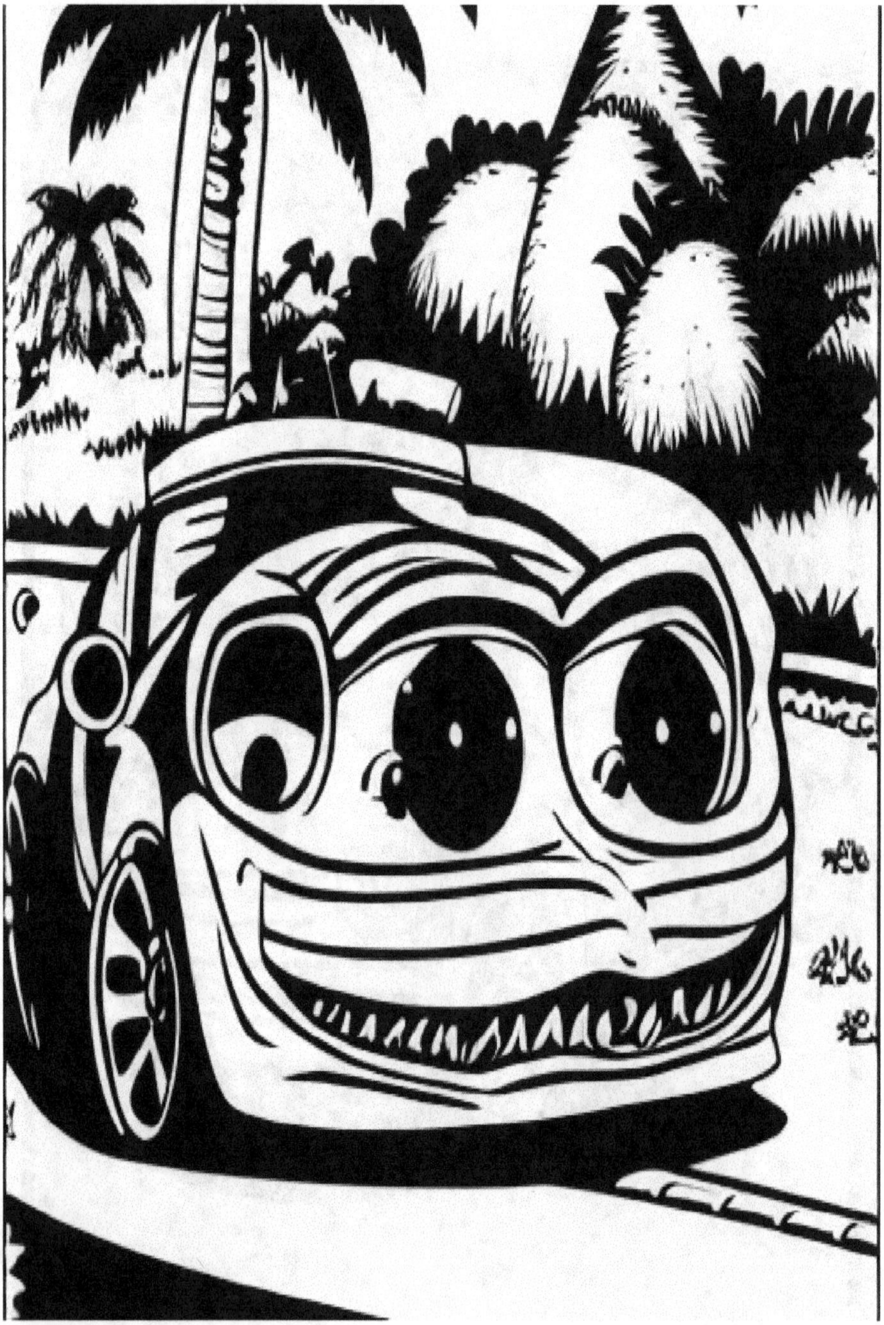

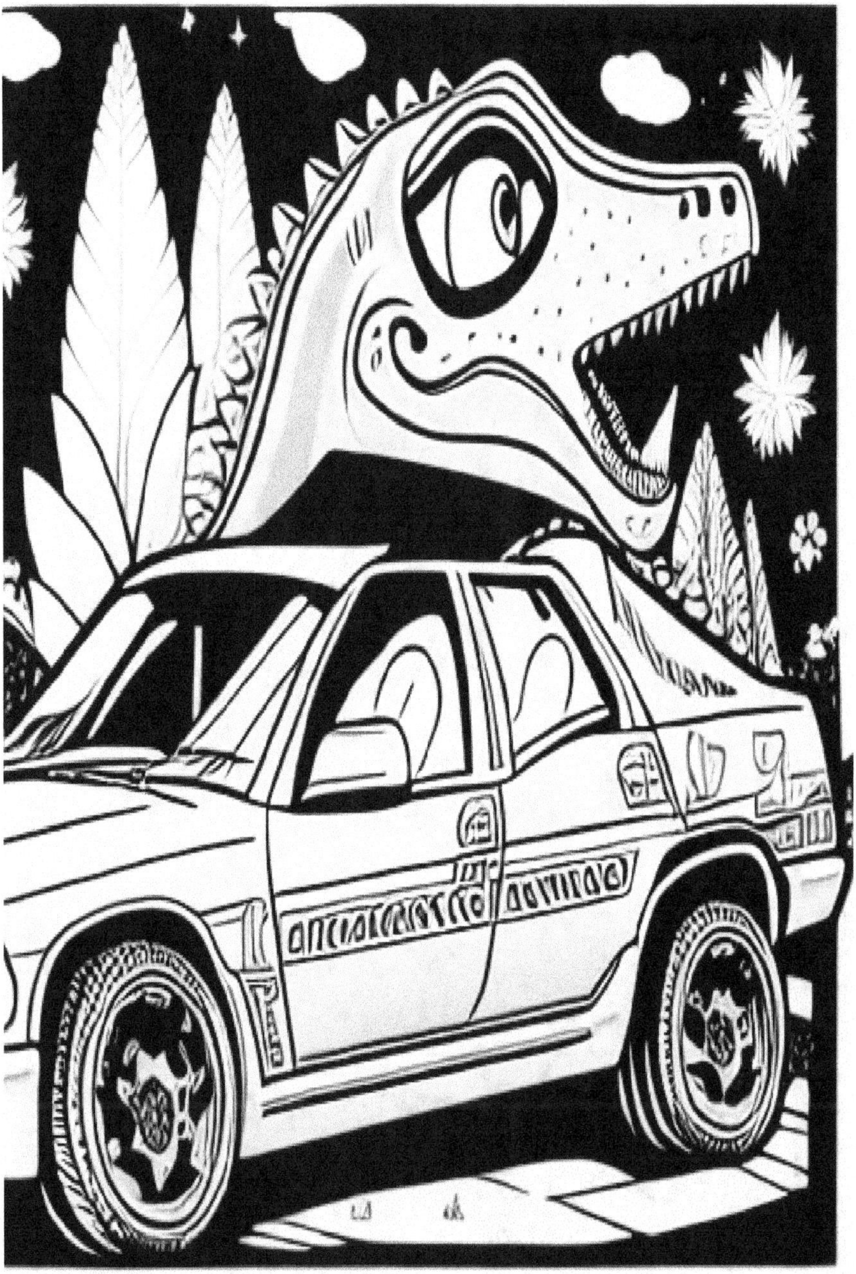

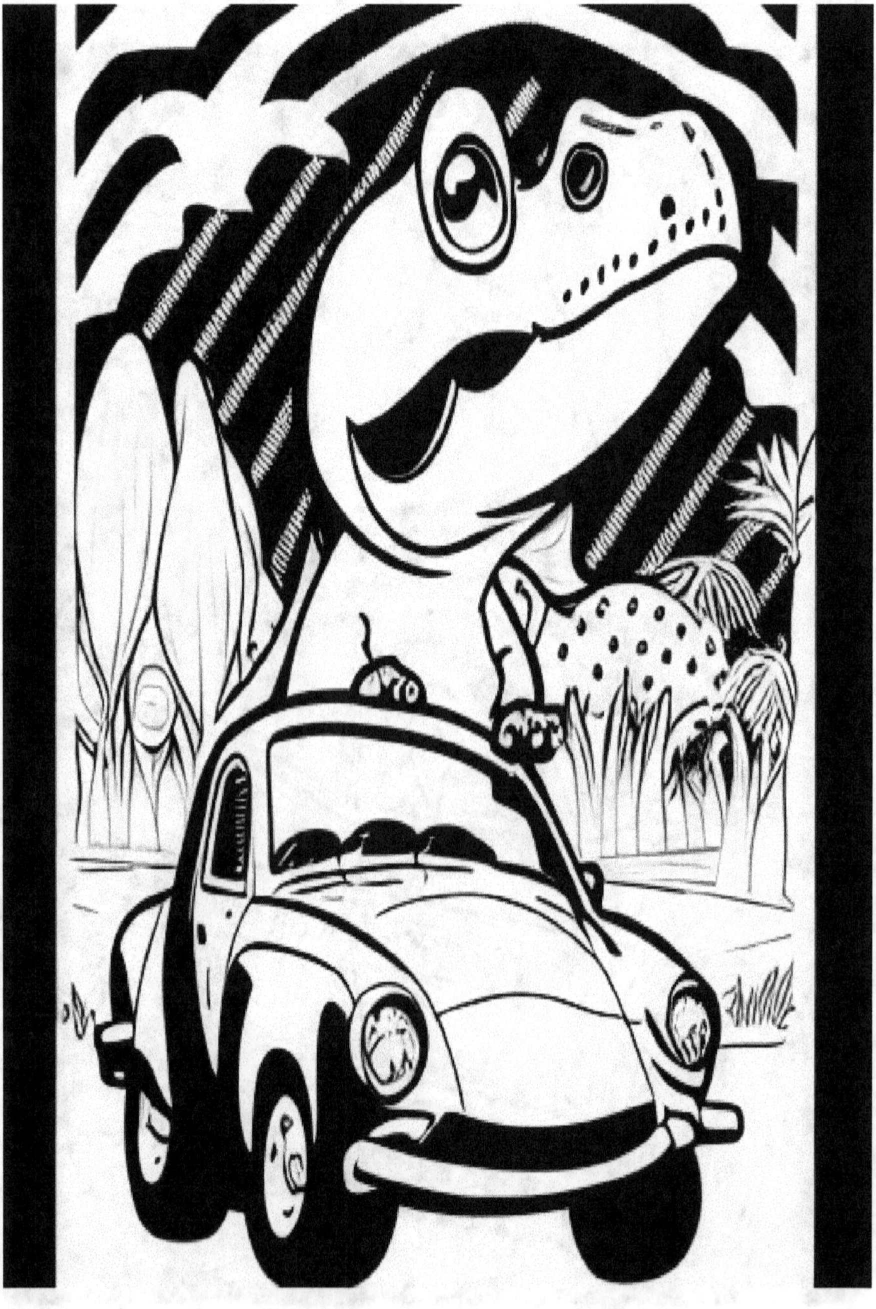

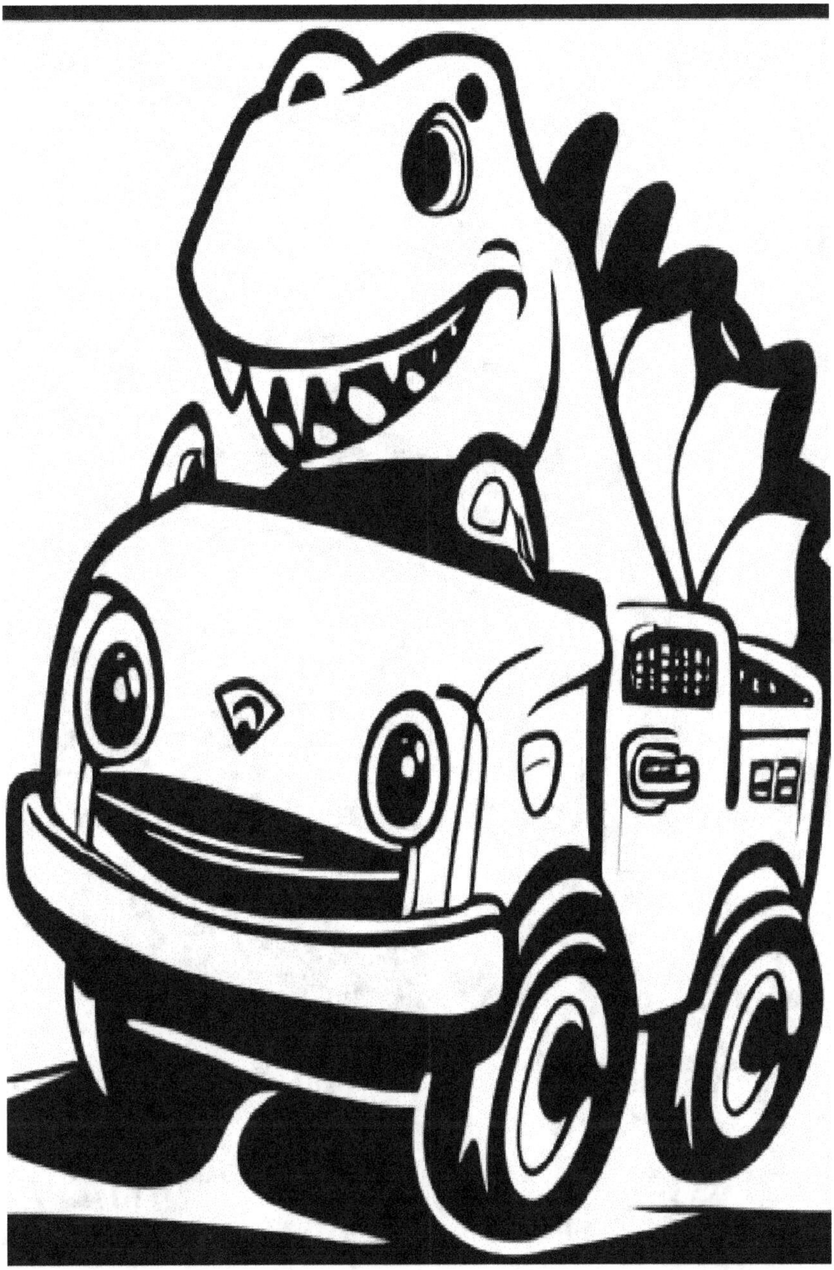

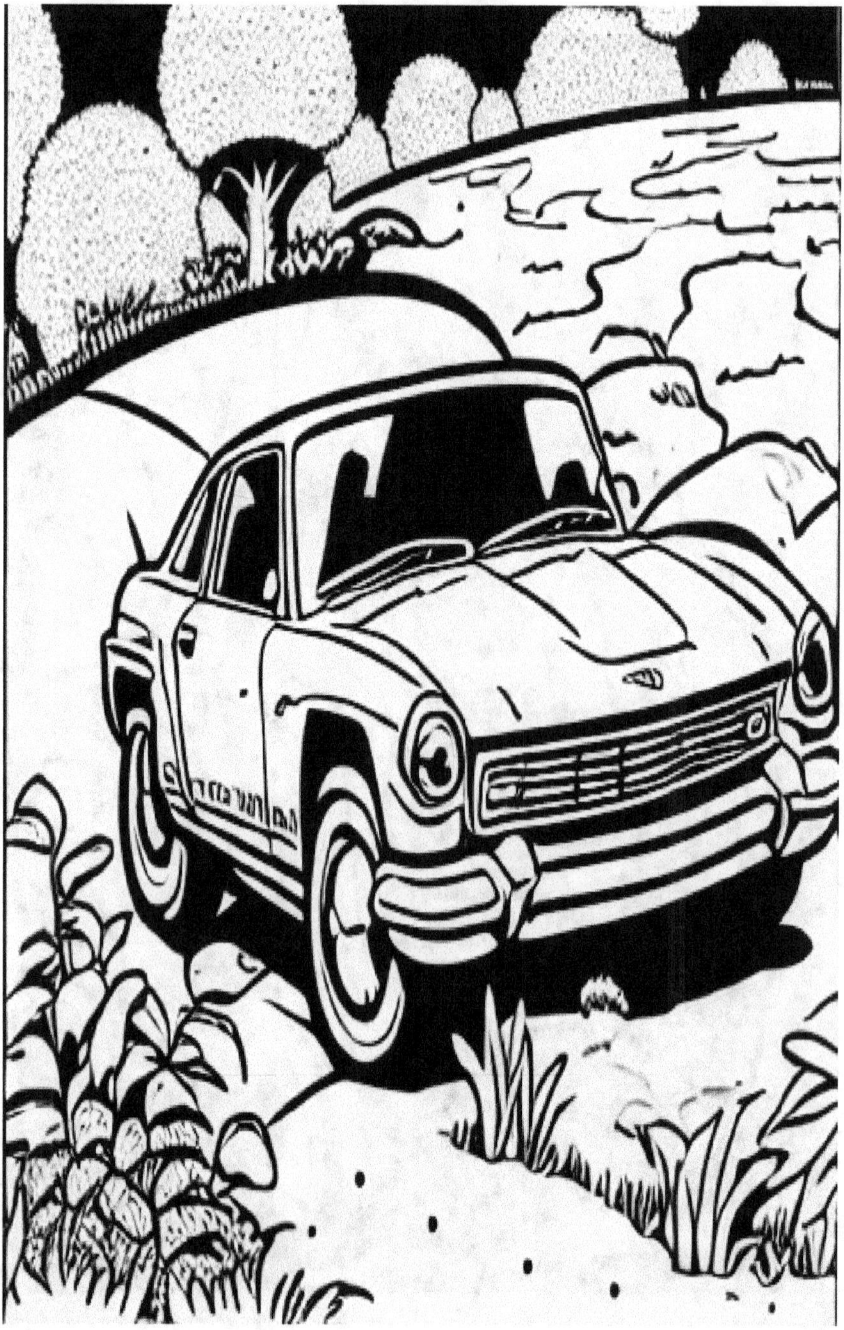

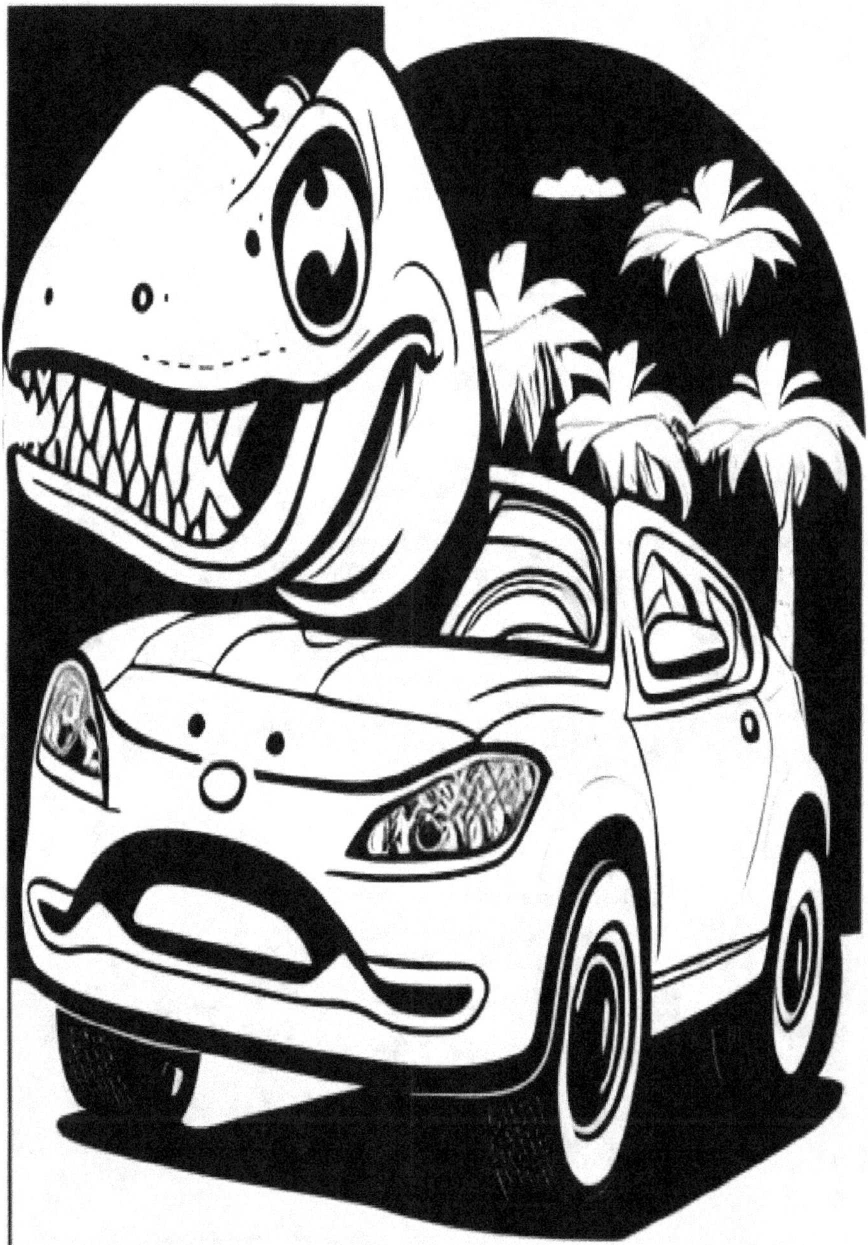

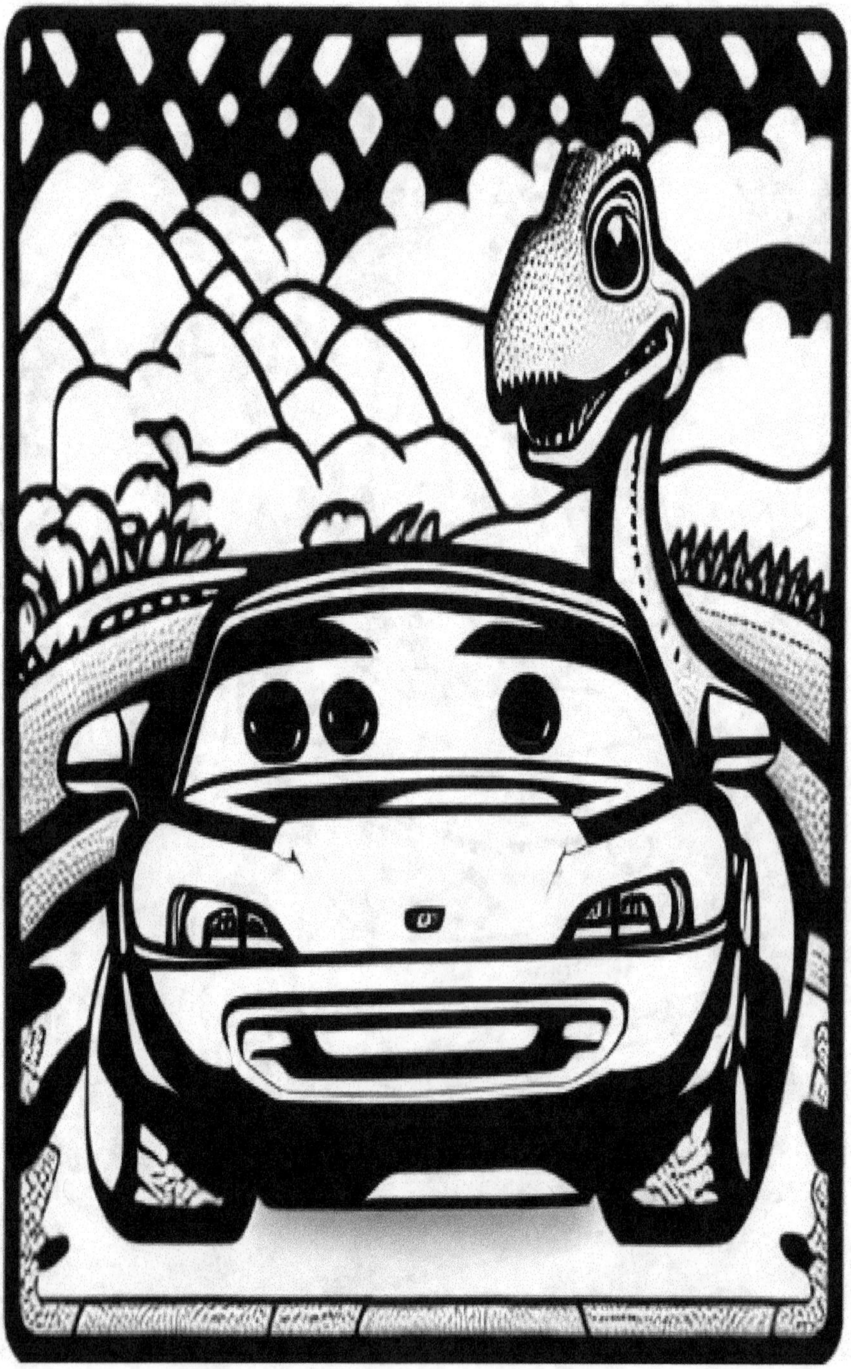

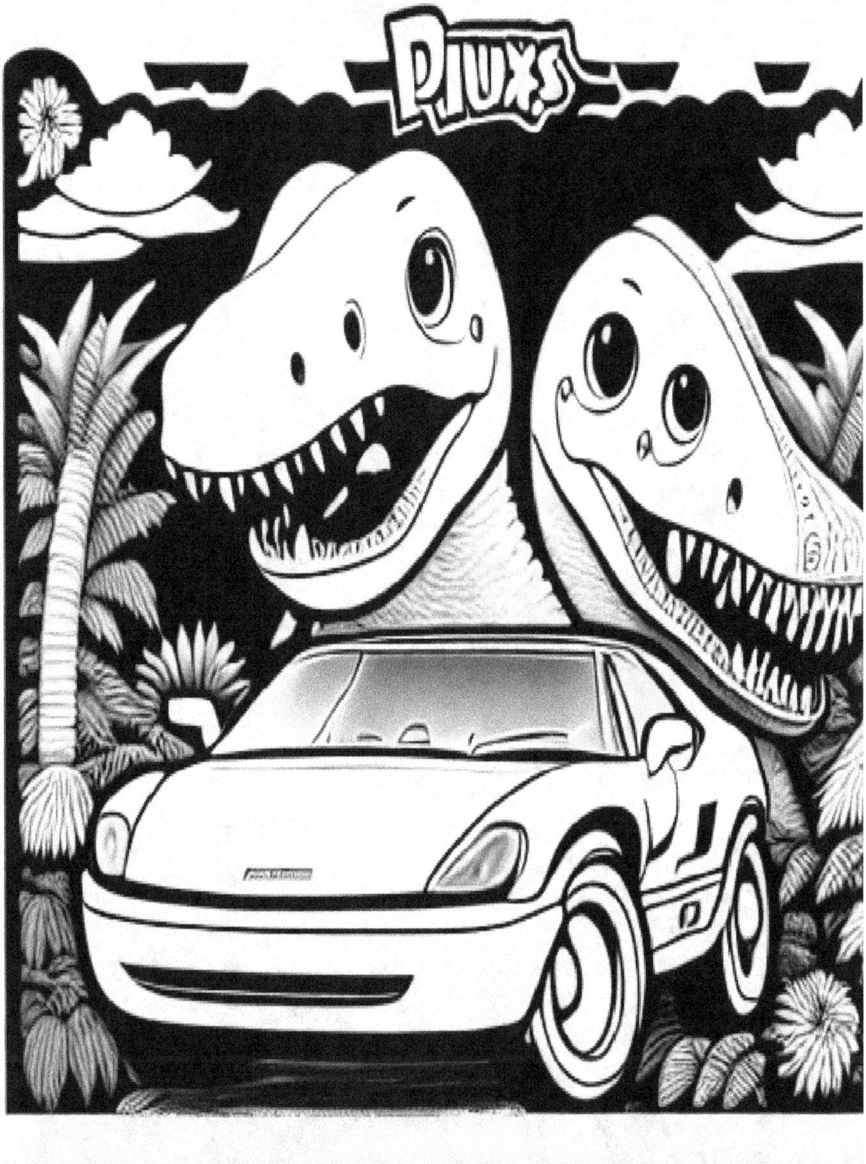

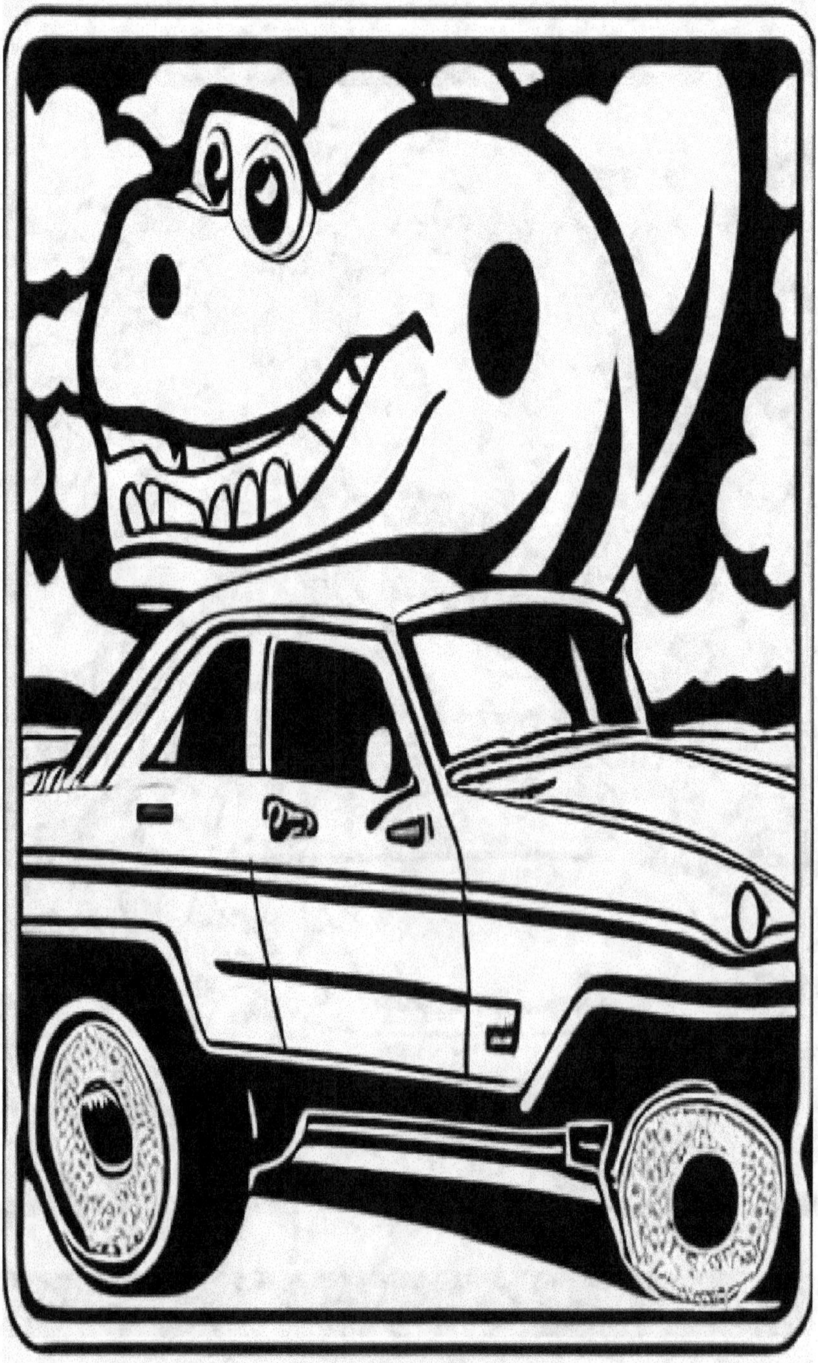

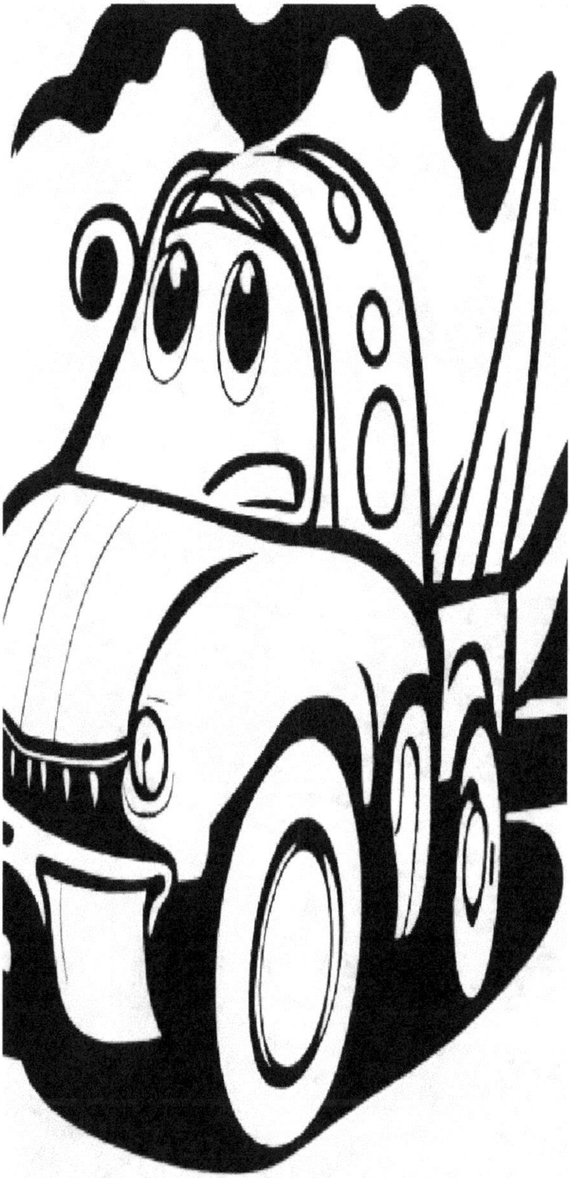

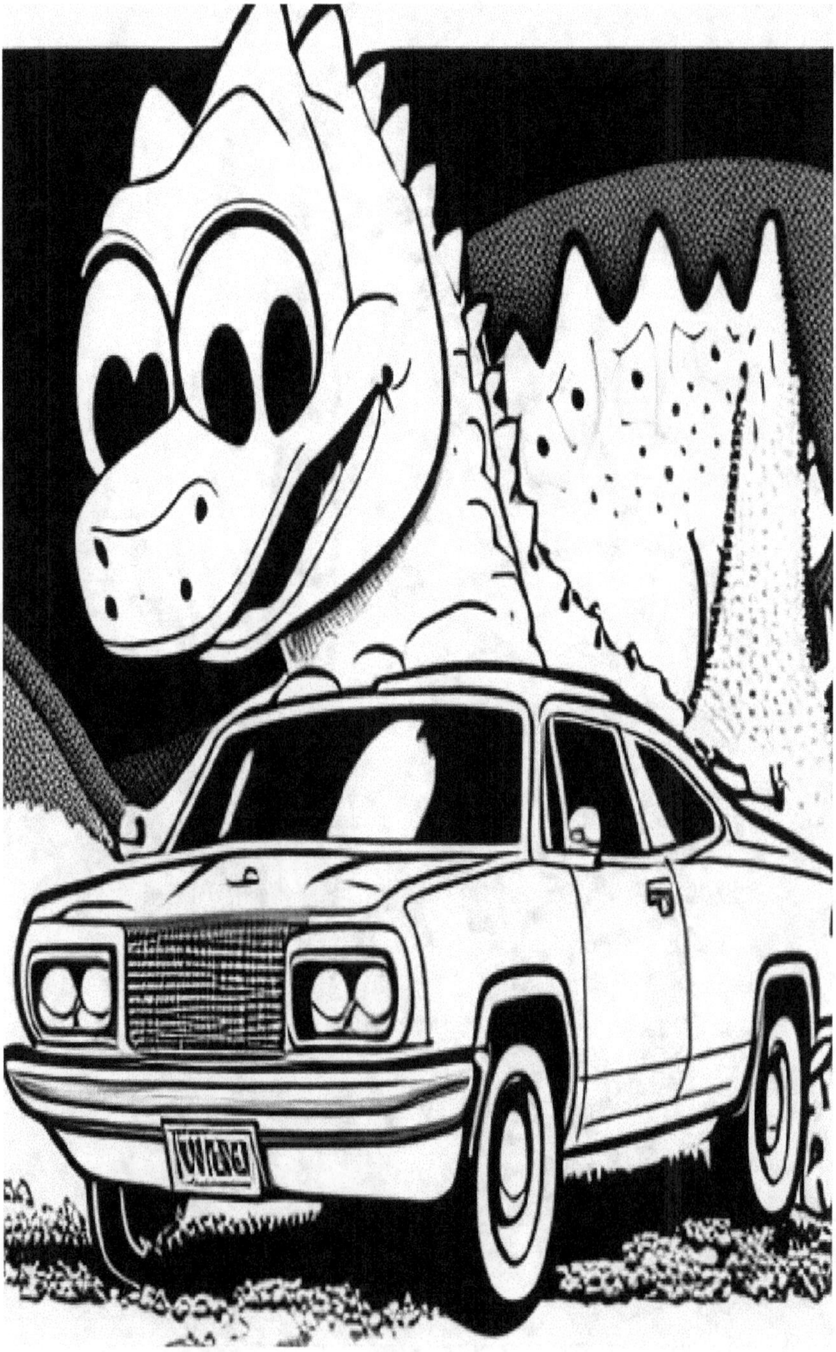

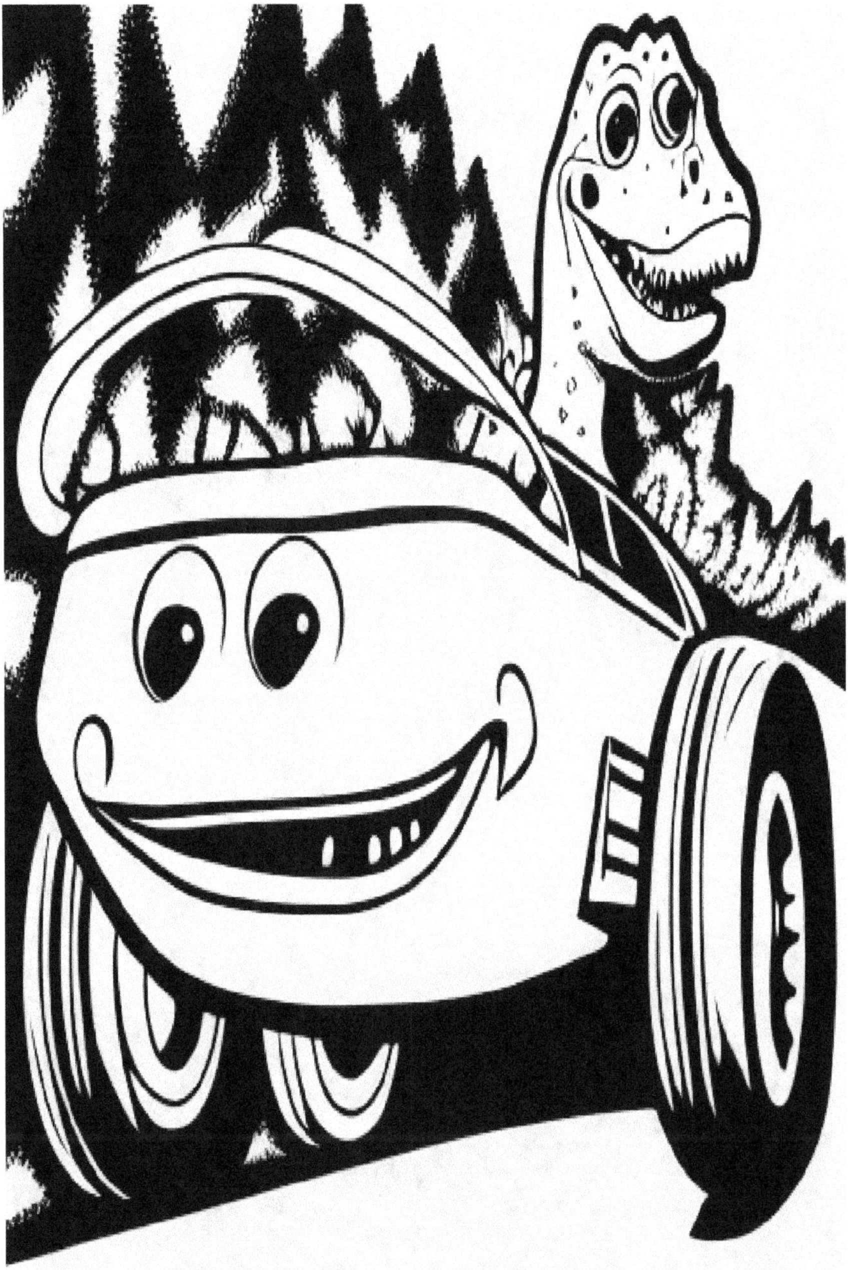

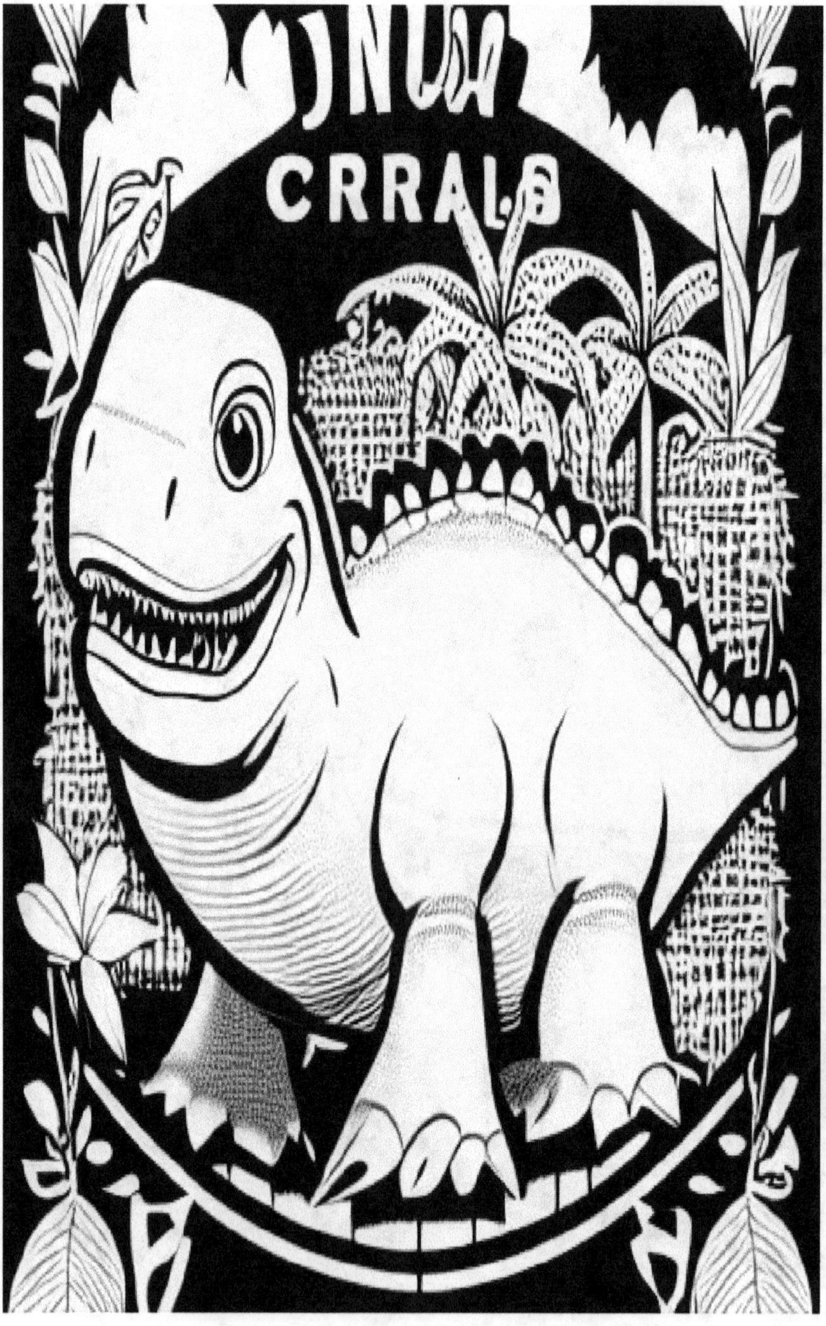
CRRALS

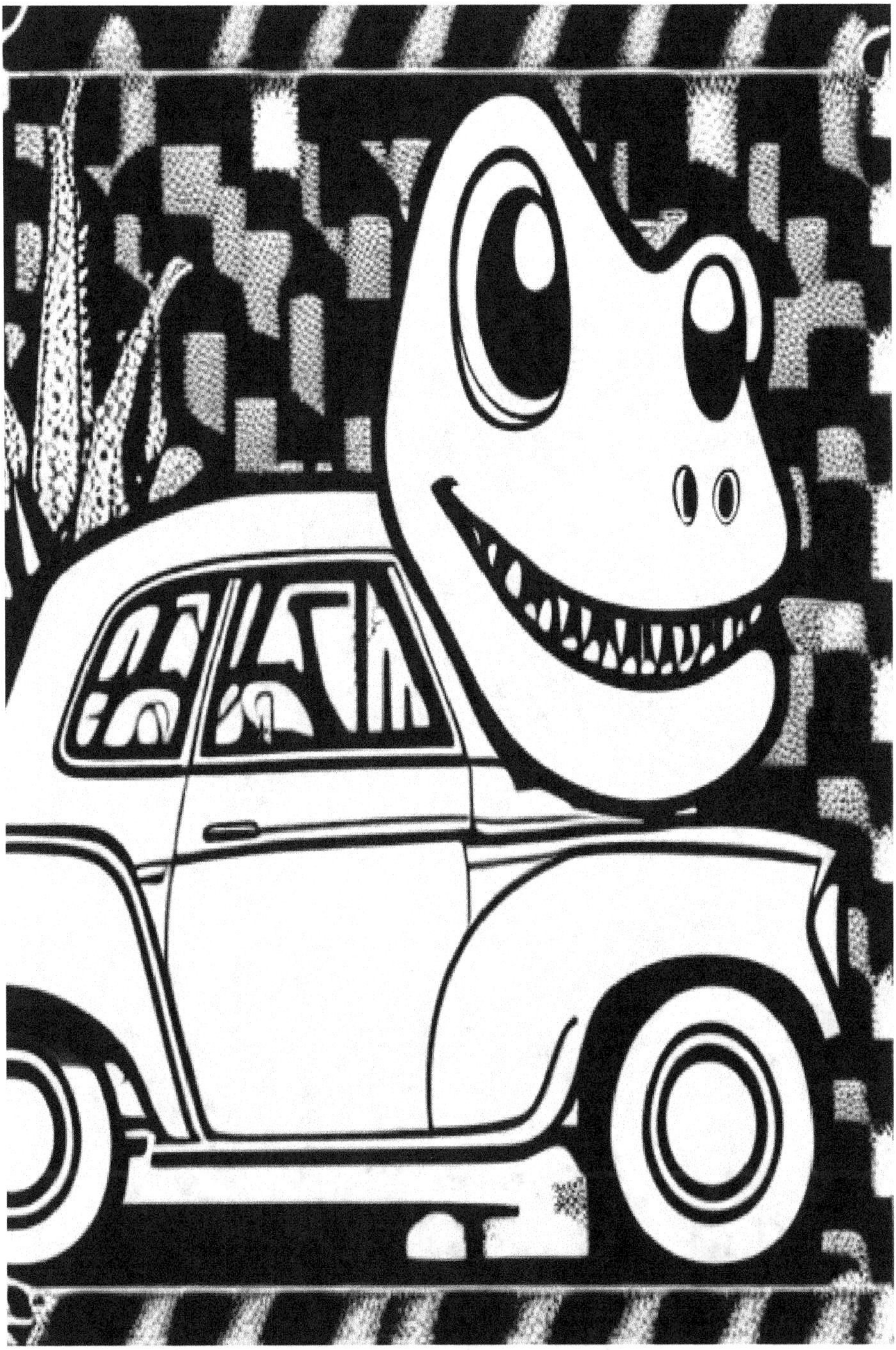

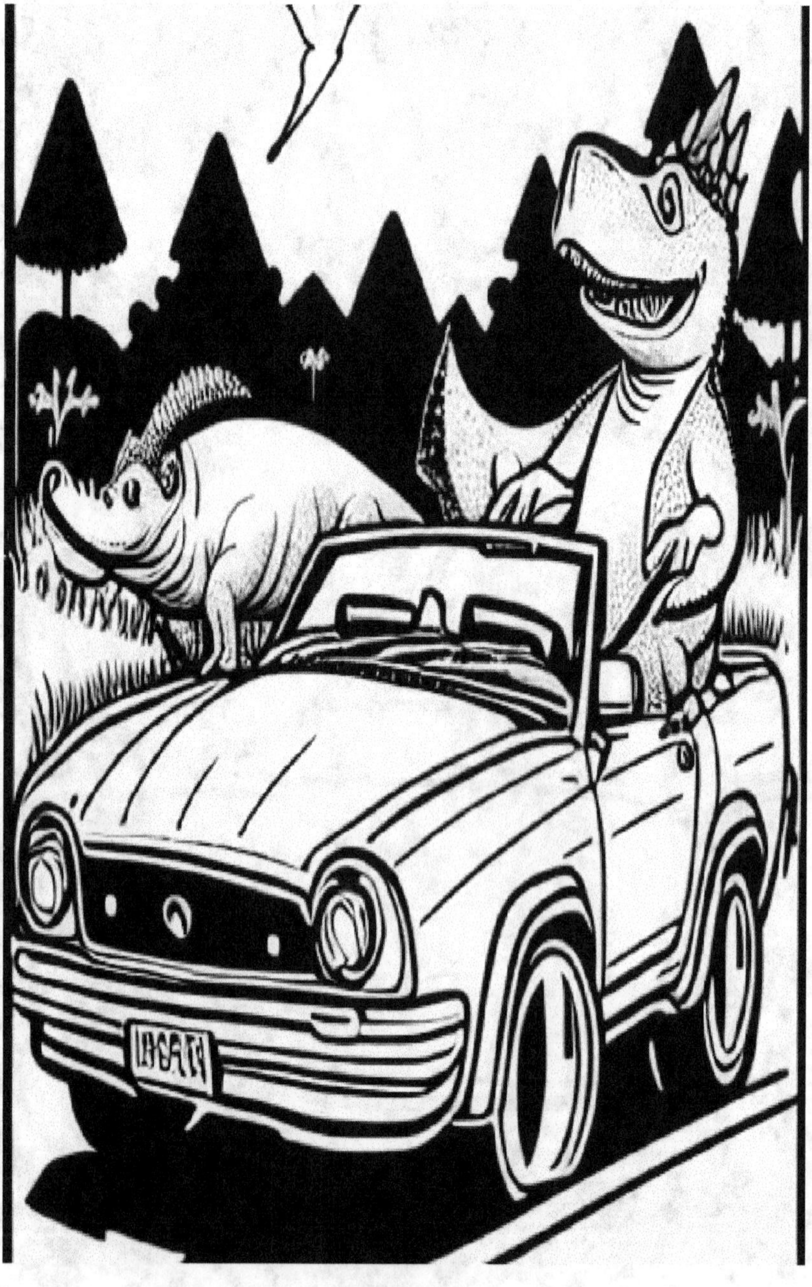

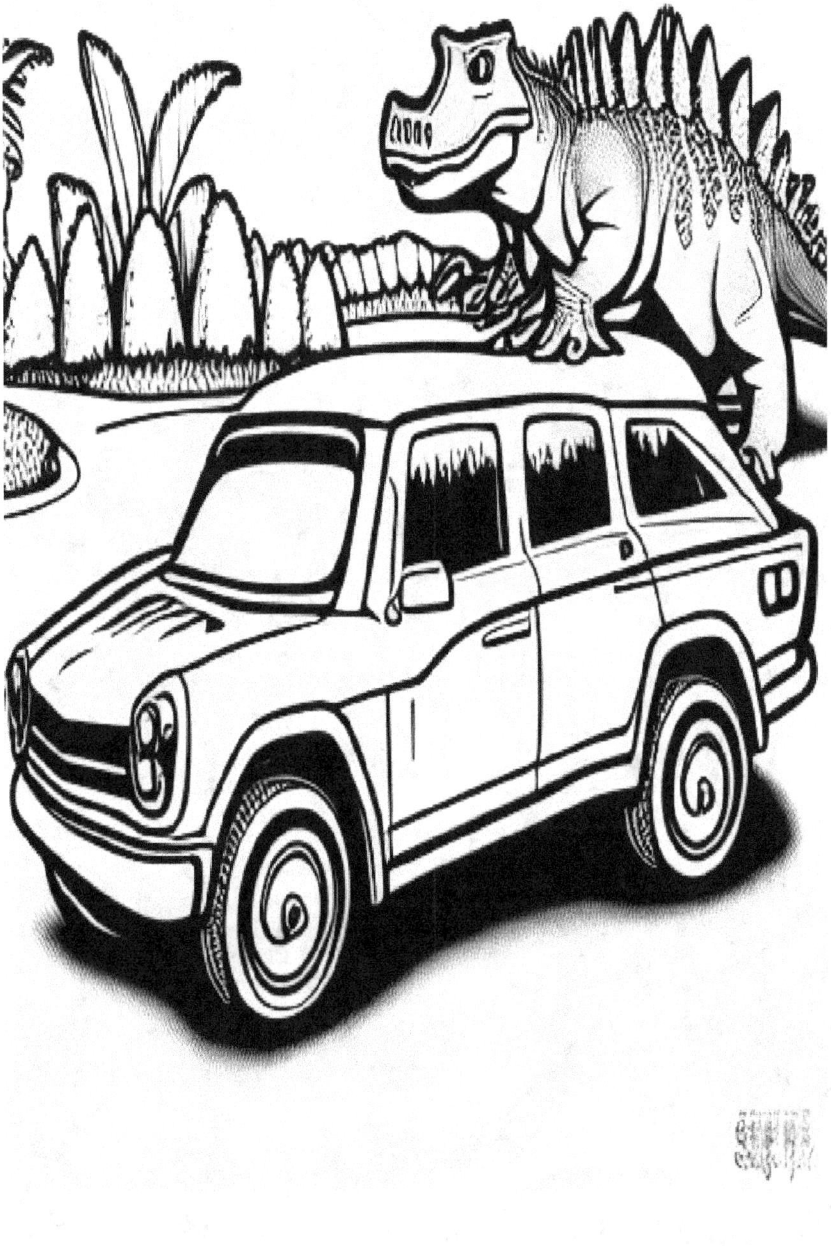

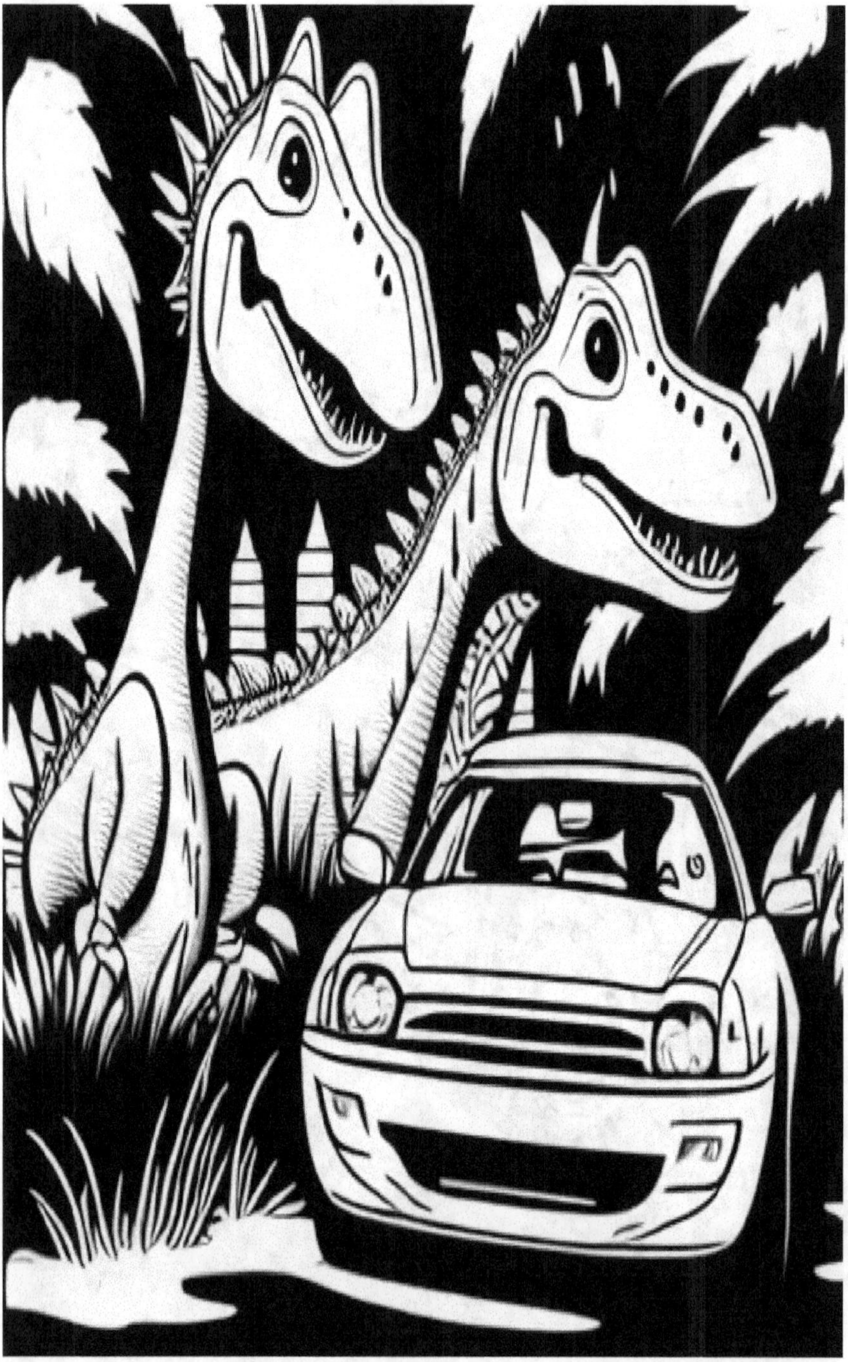

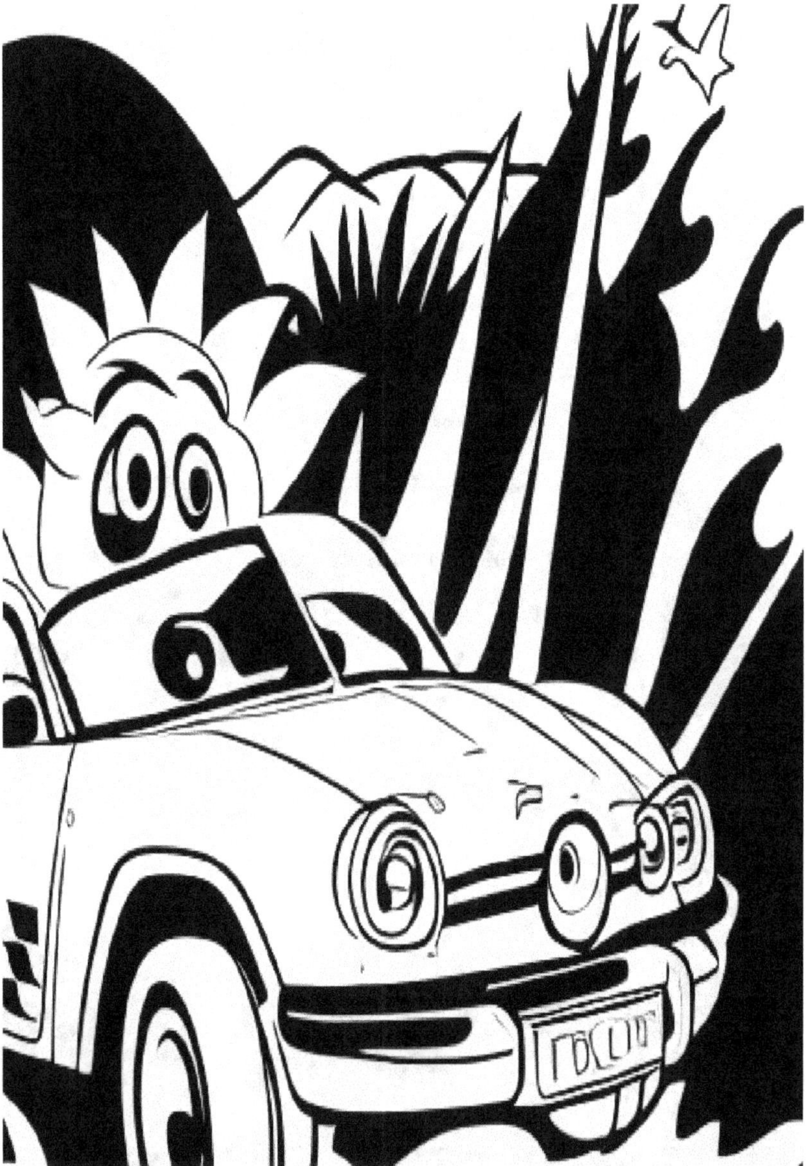

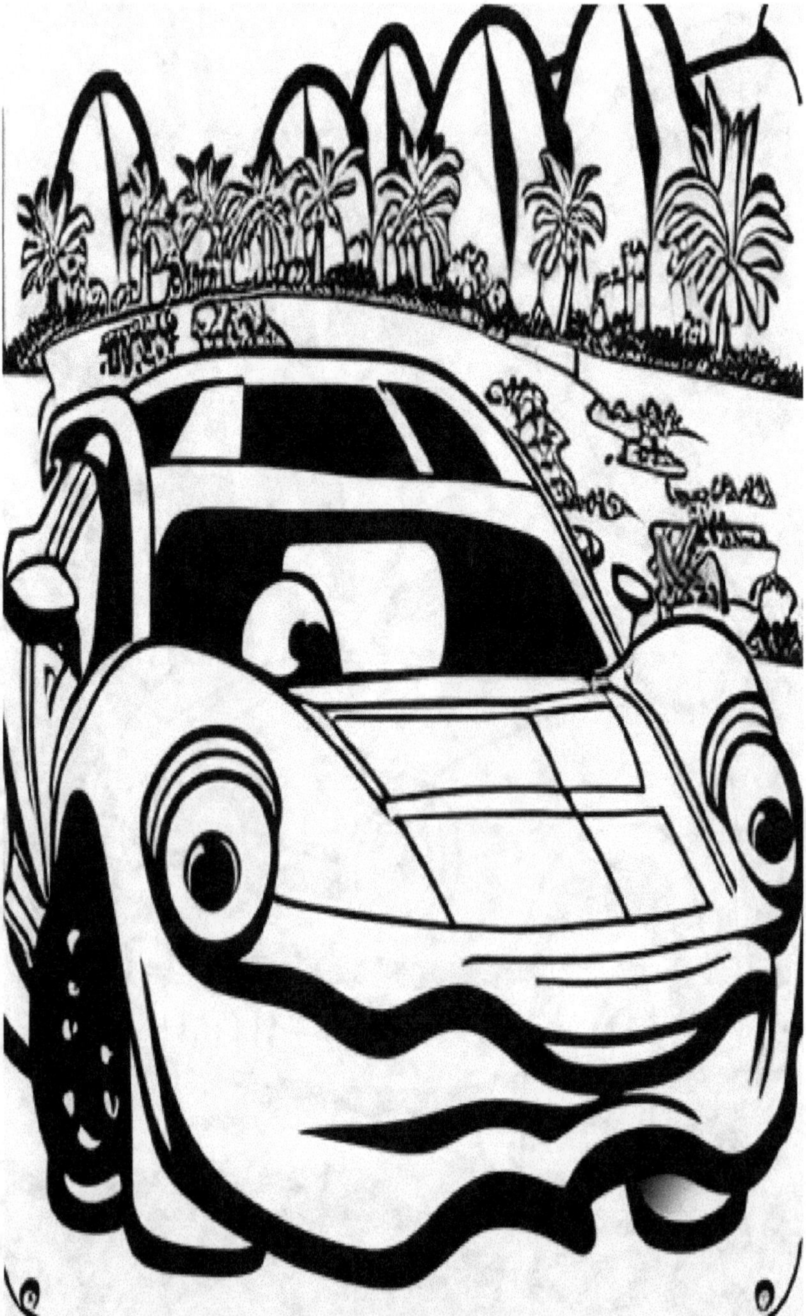

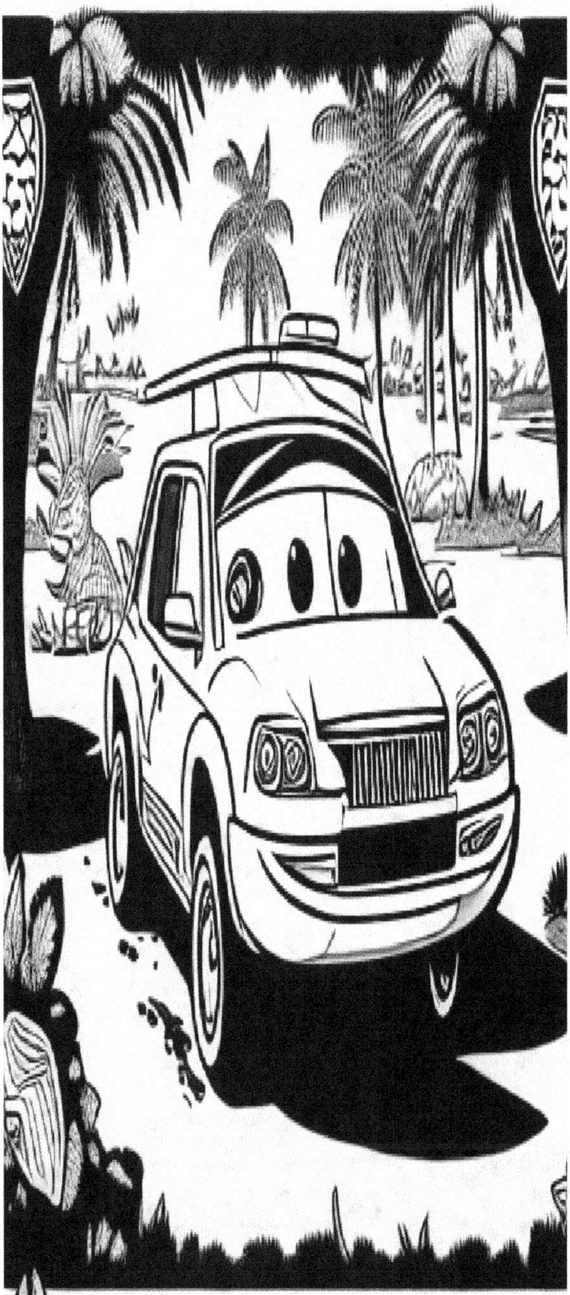

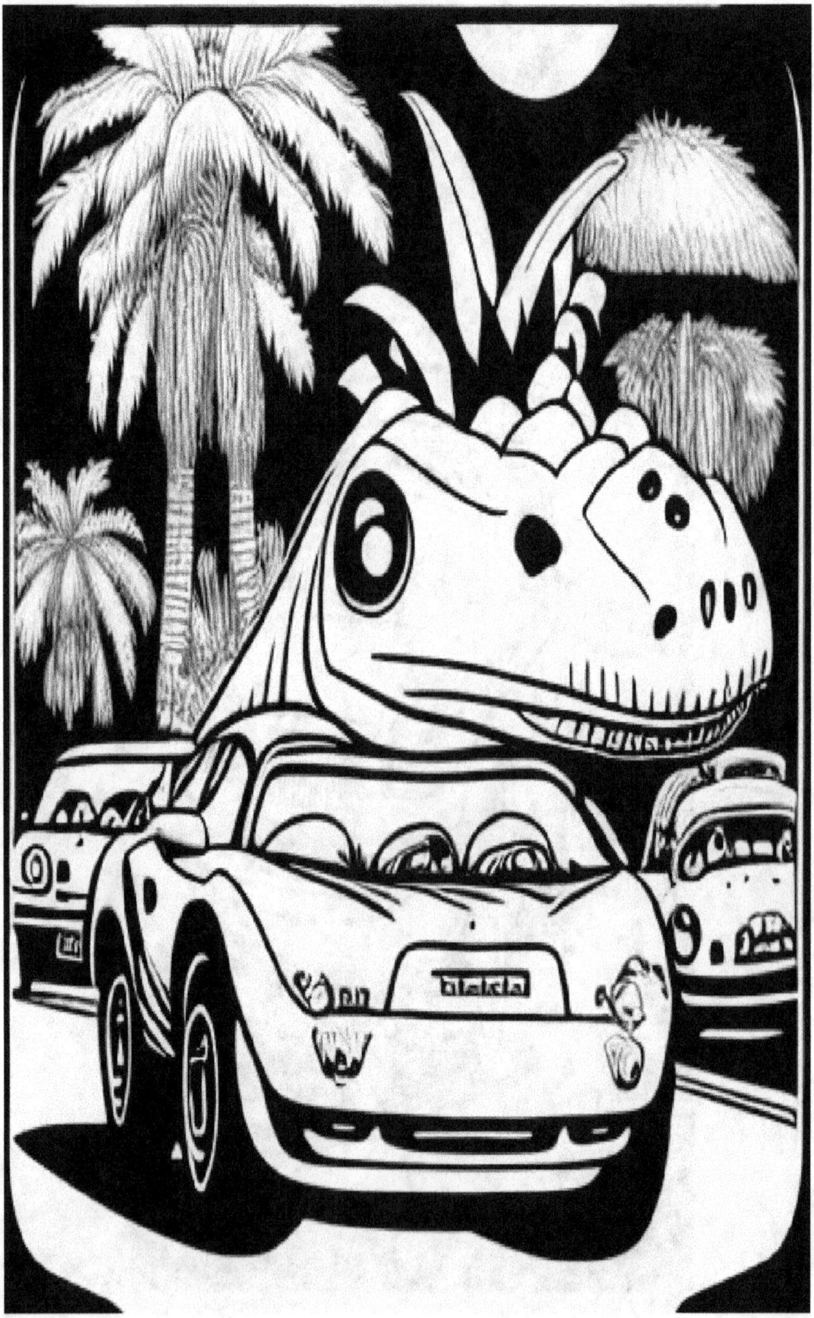

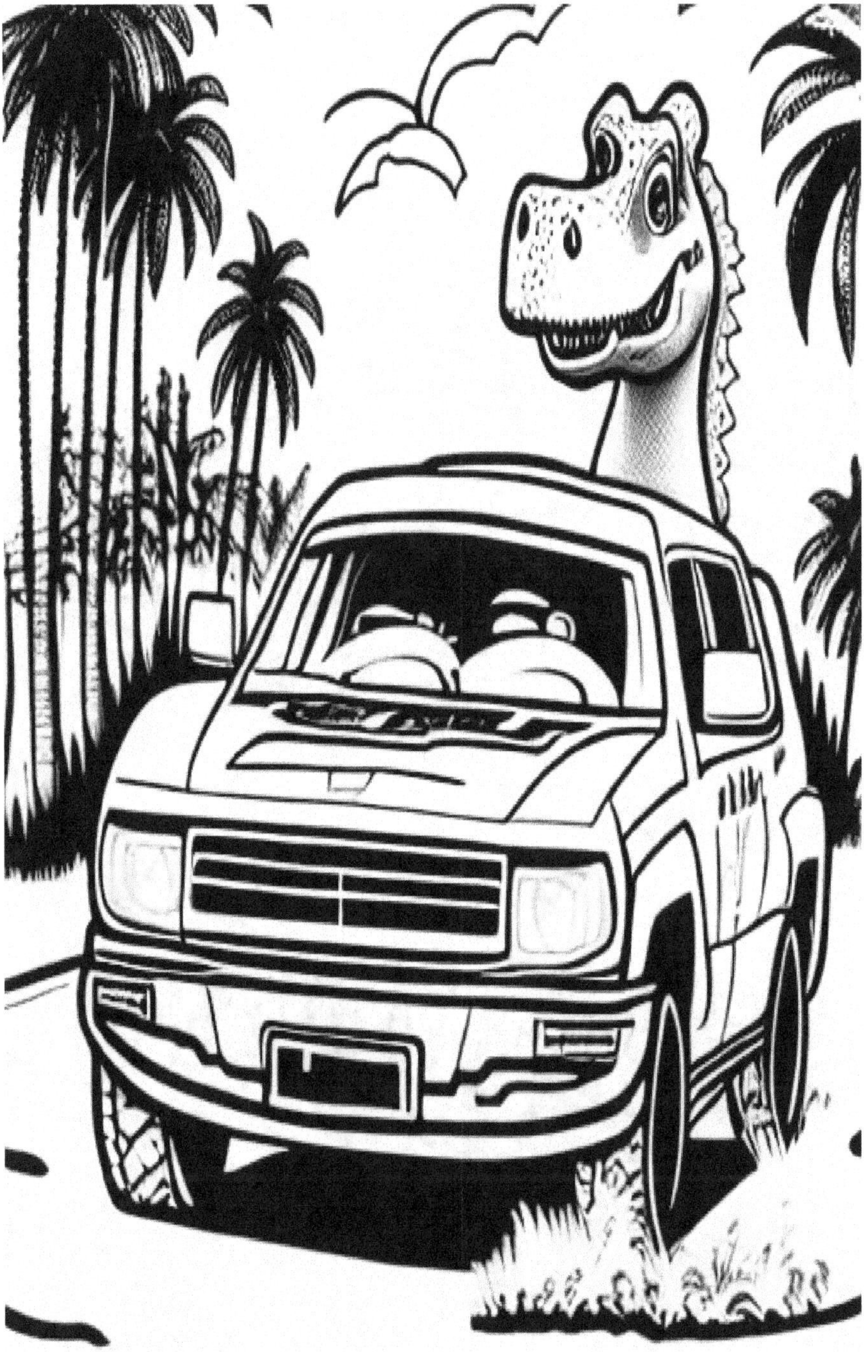

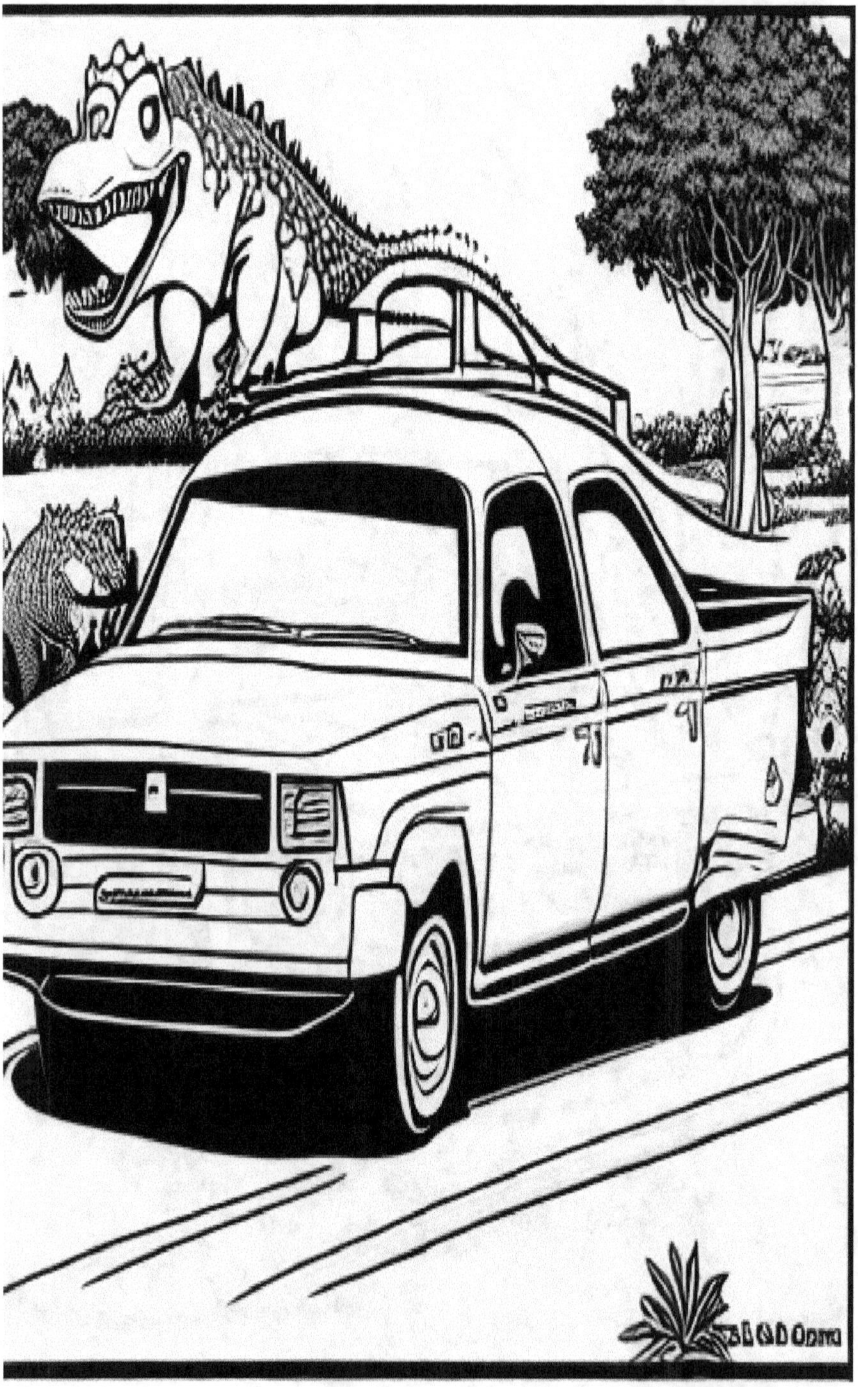

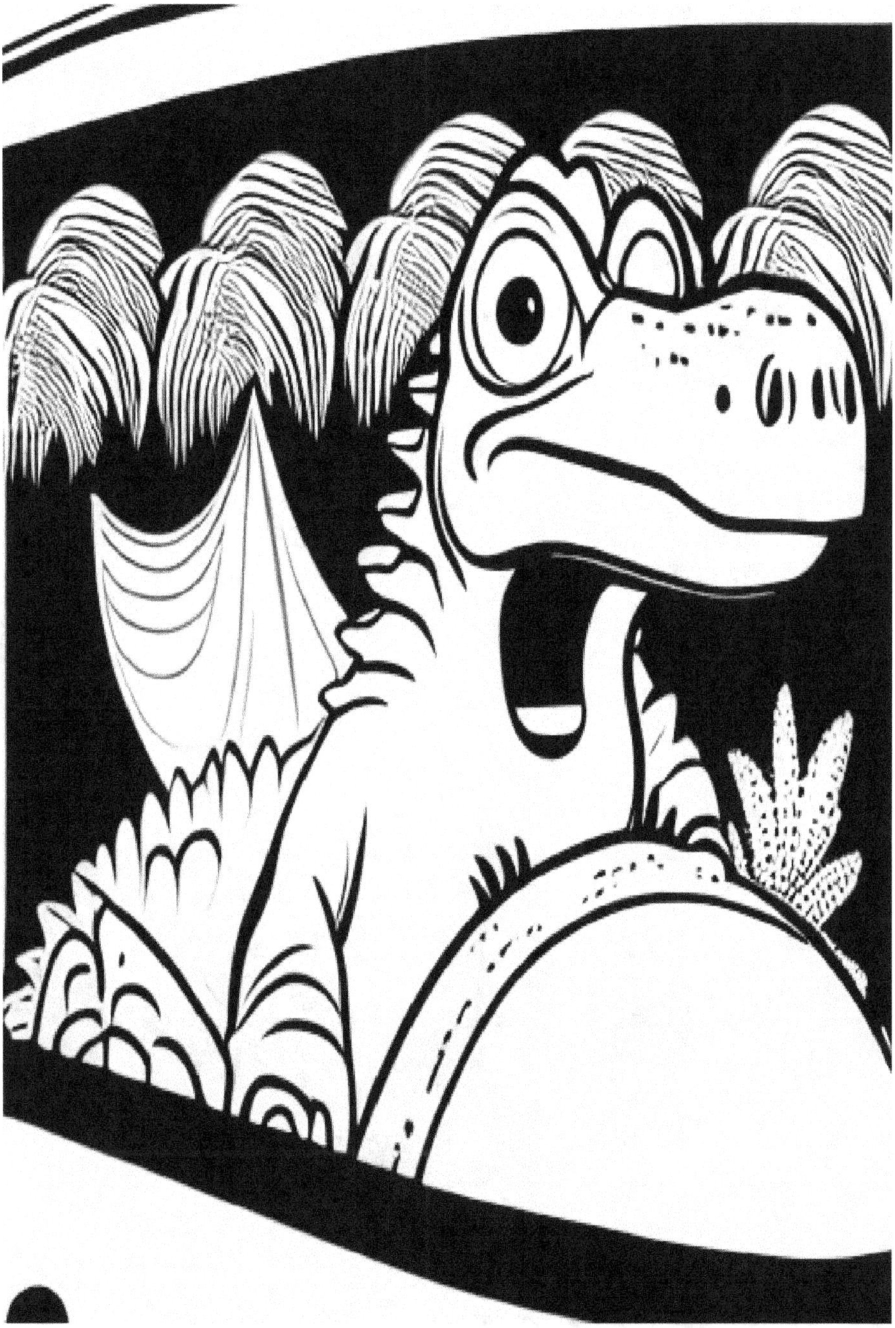

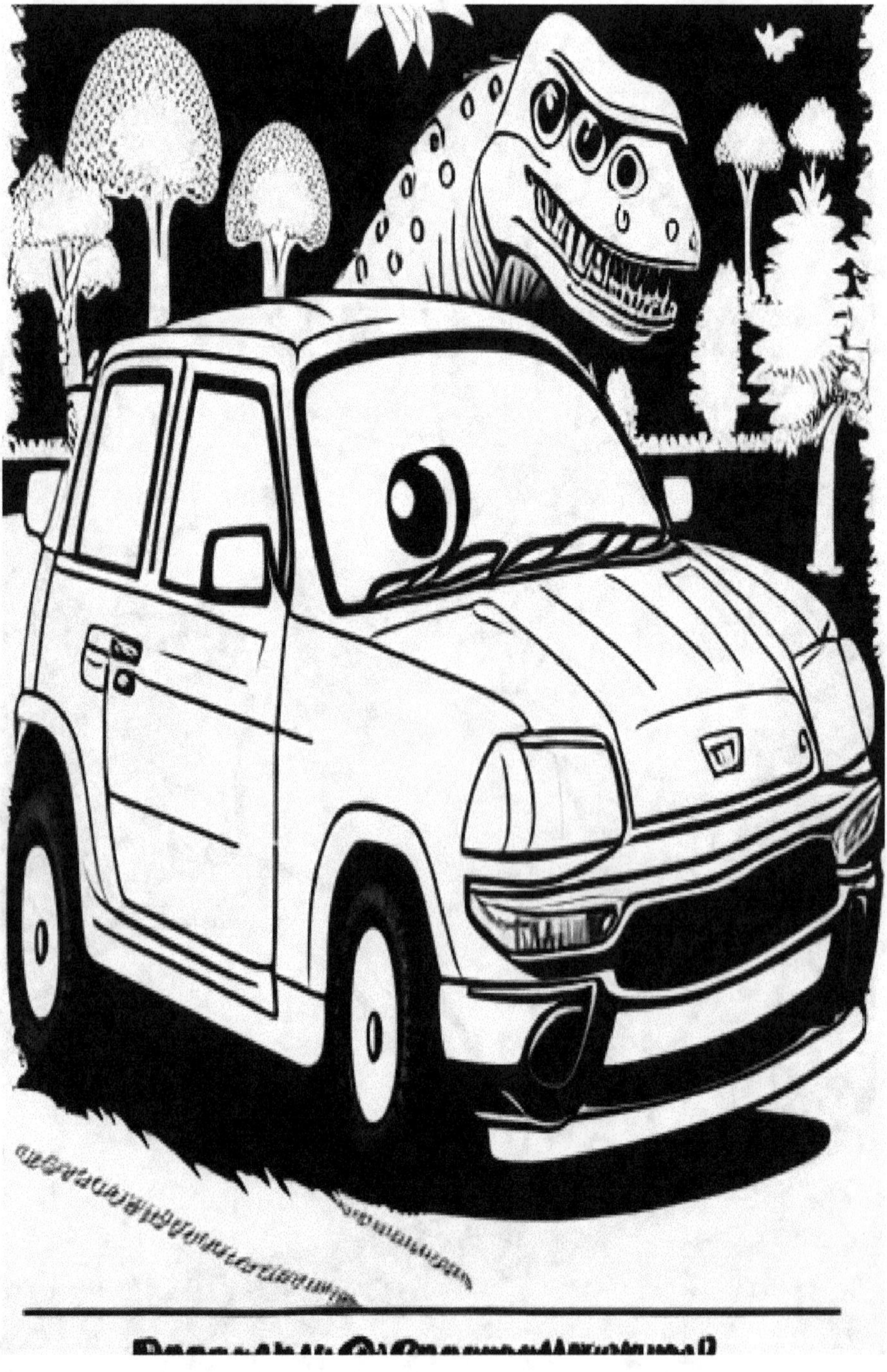

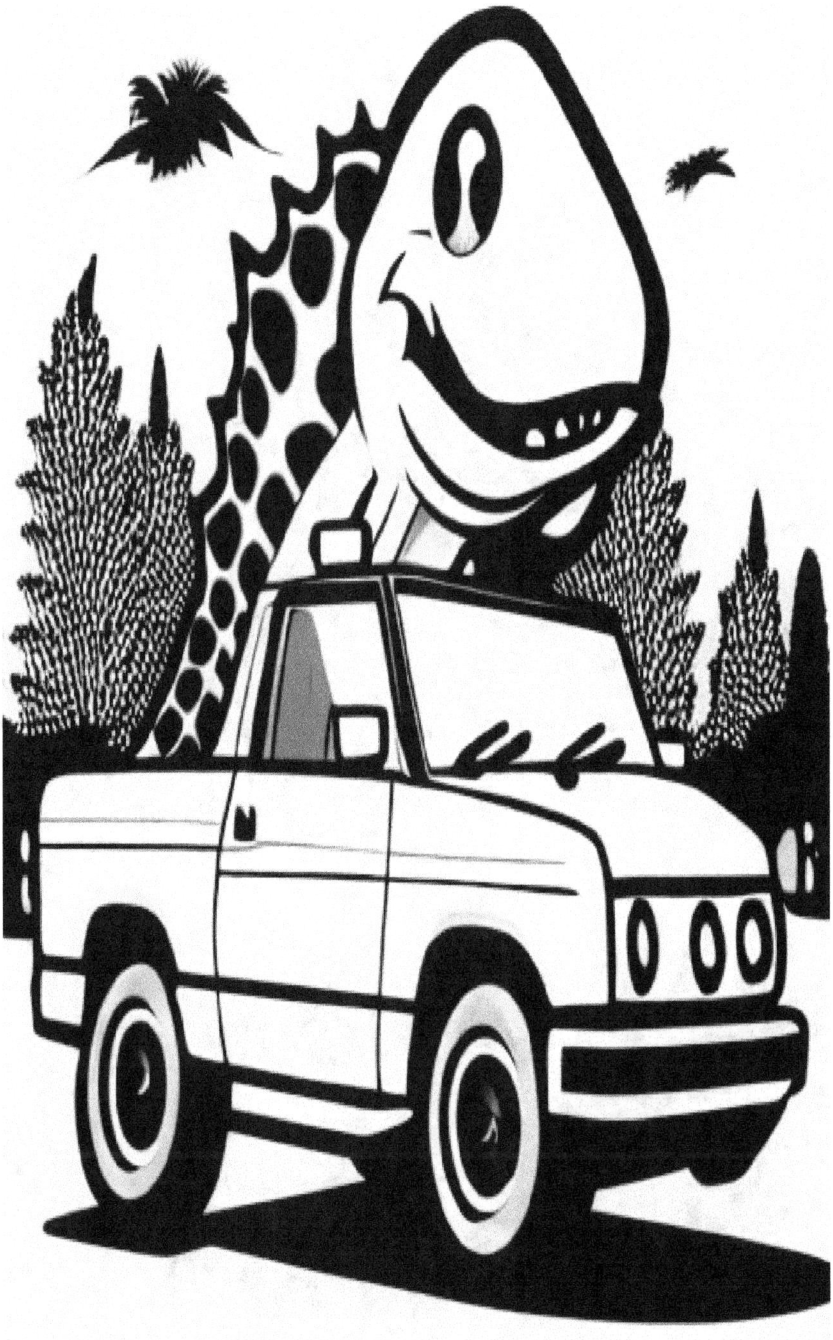

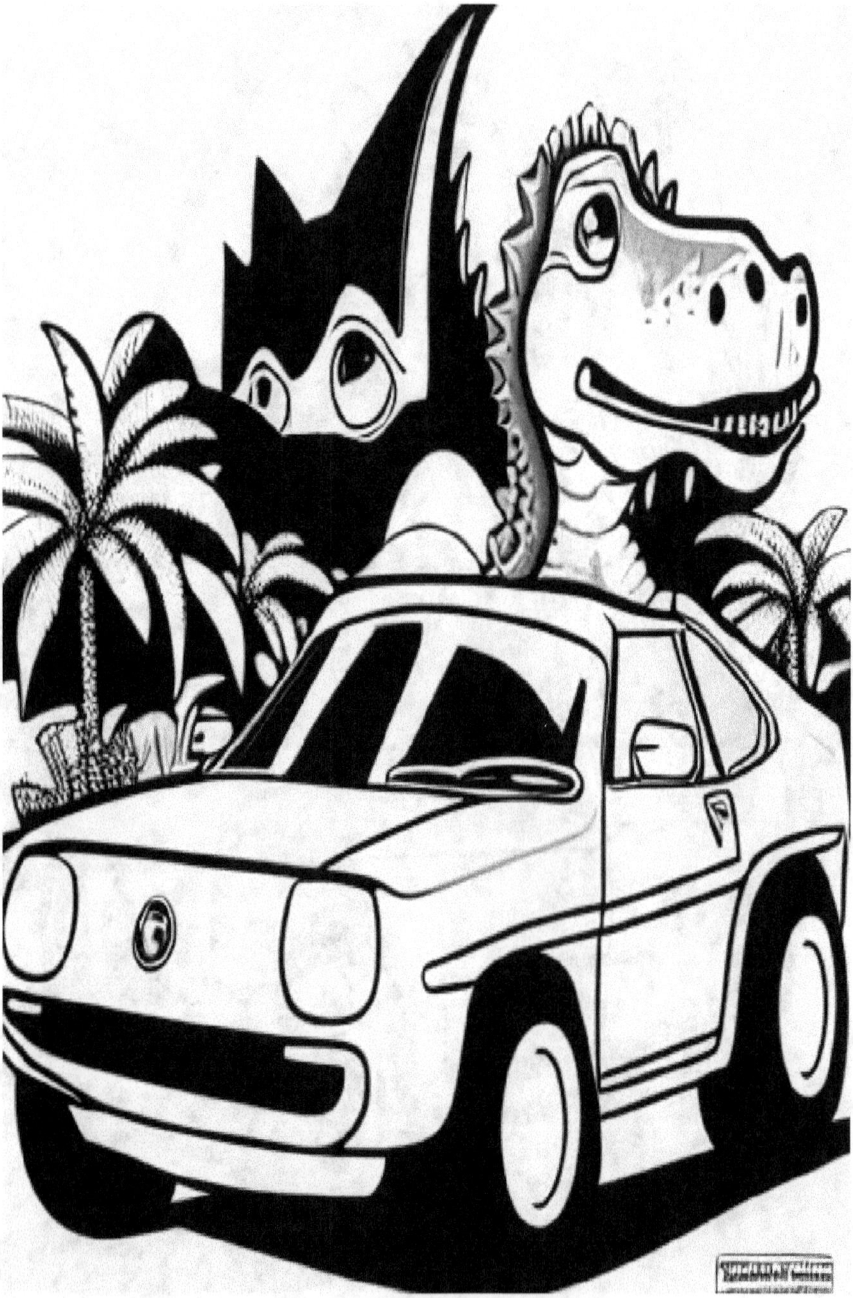

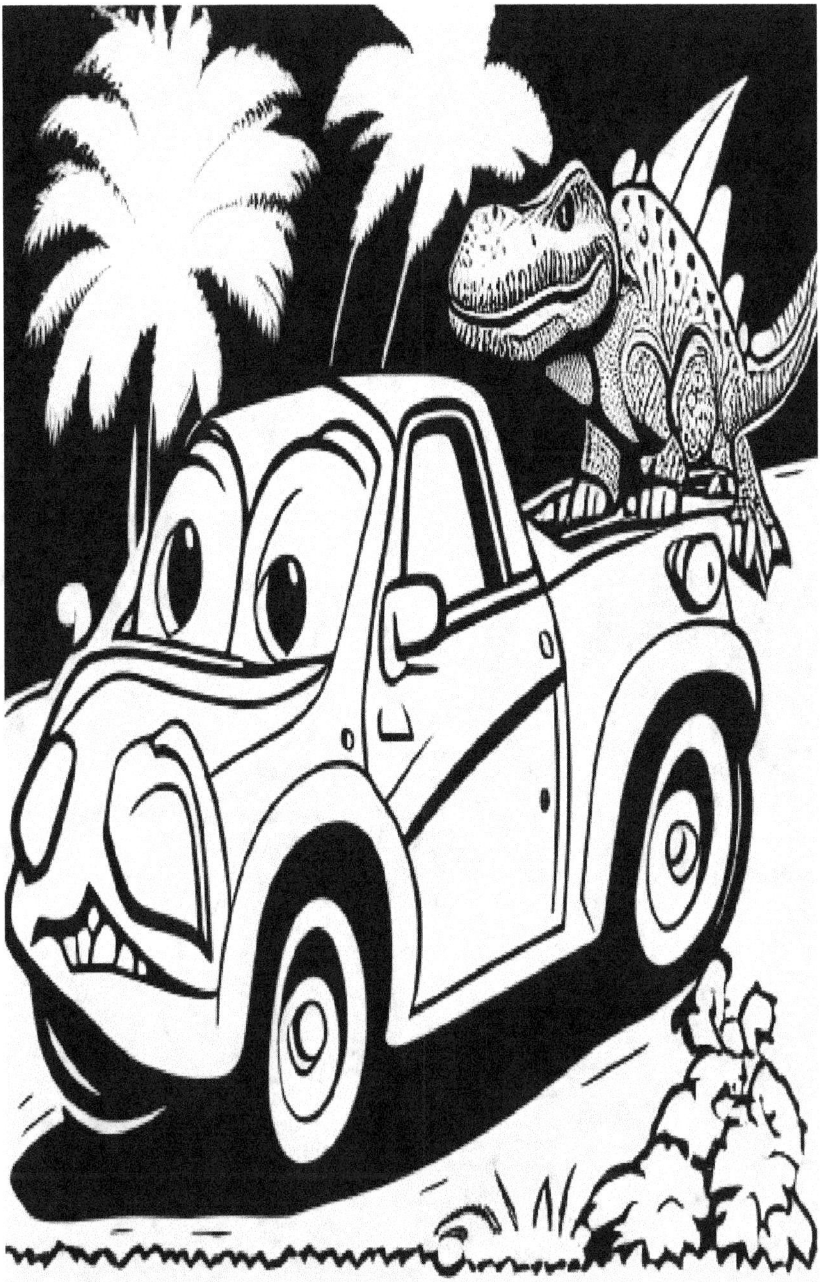

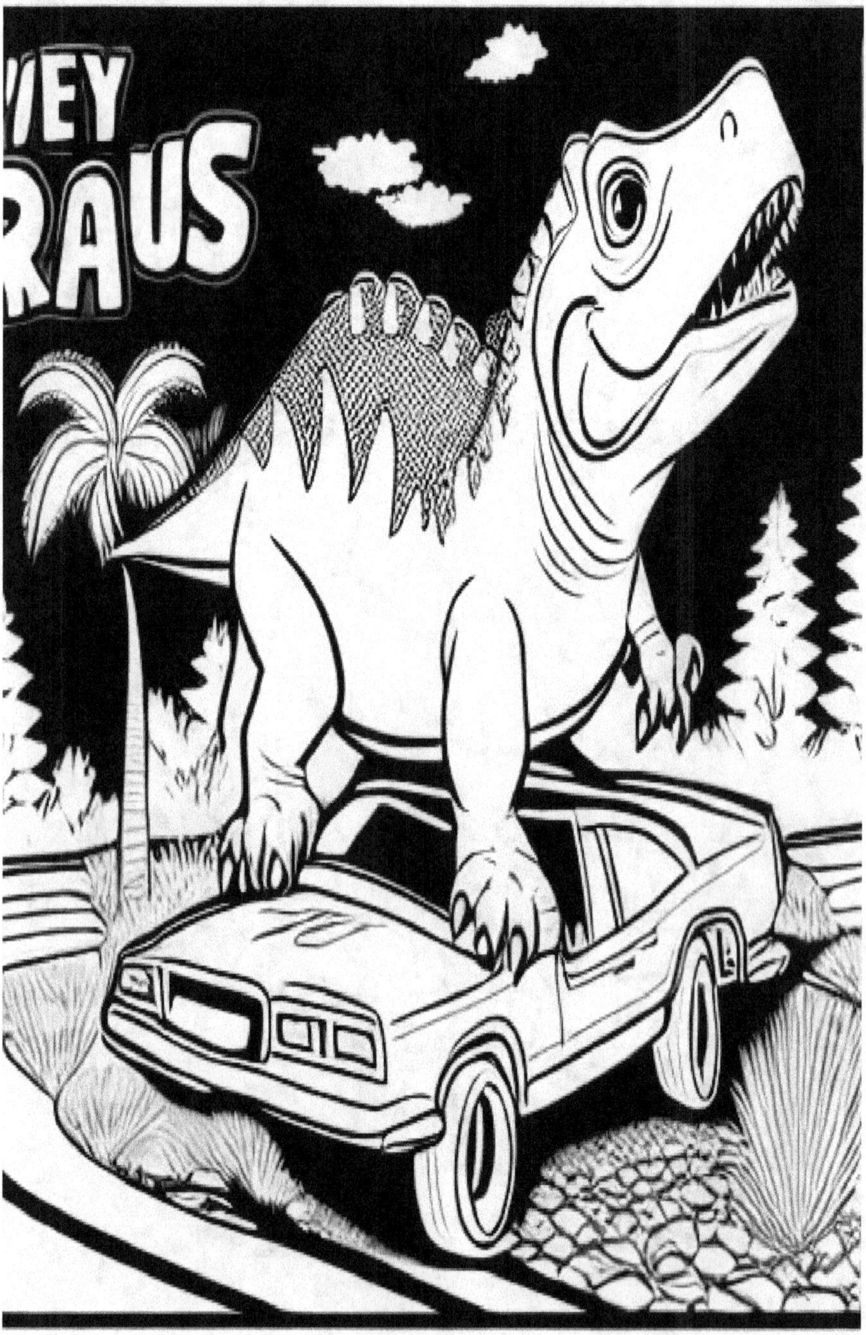
VEY
RAUS

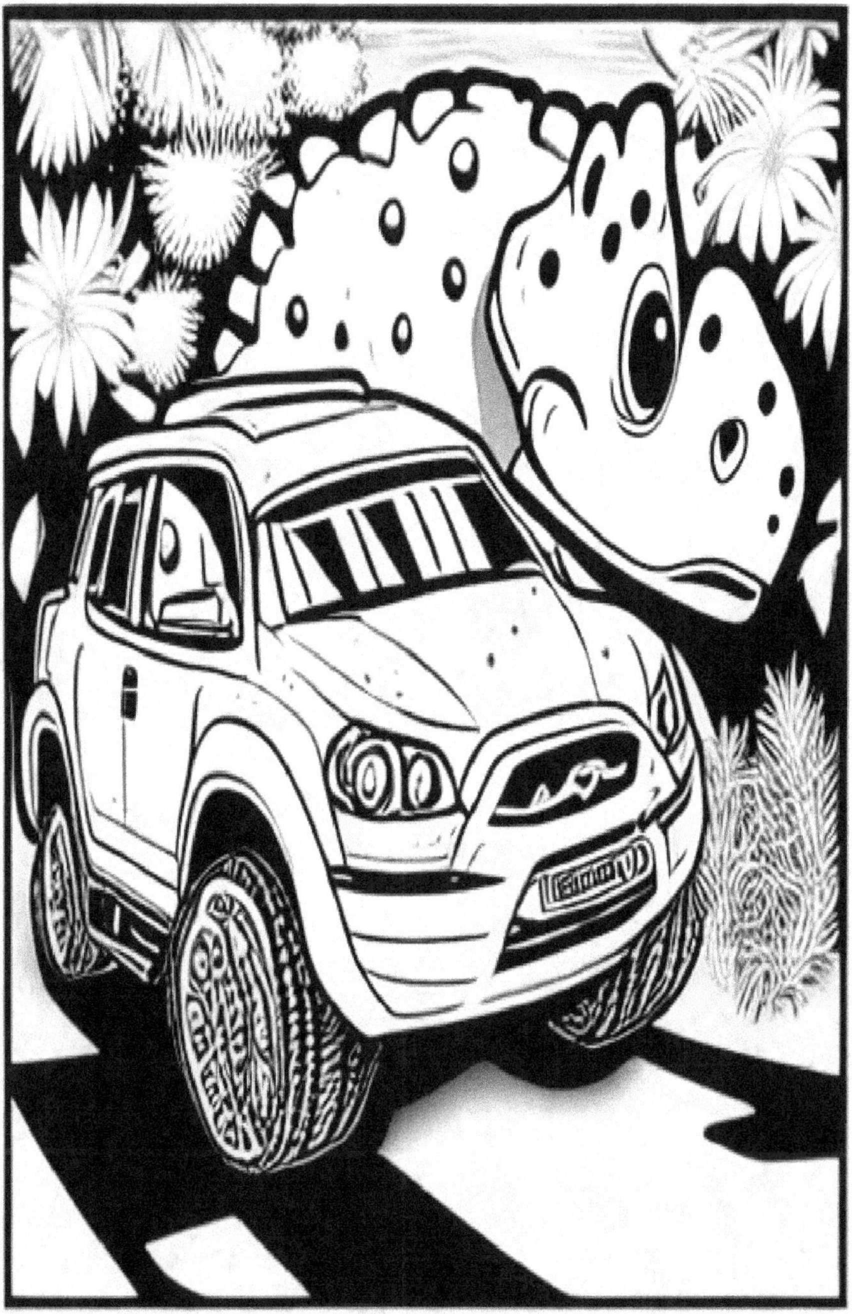

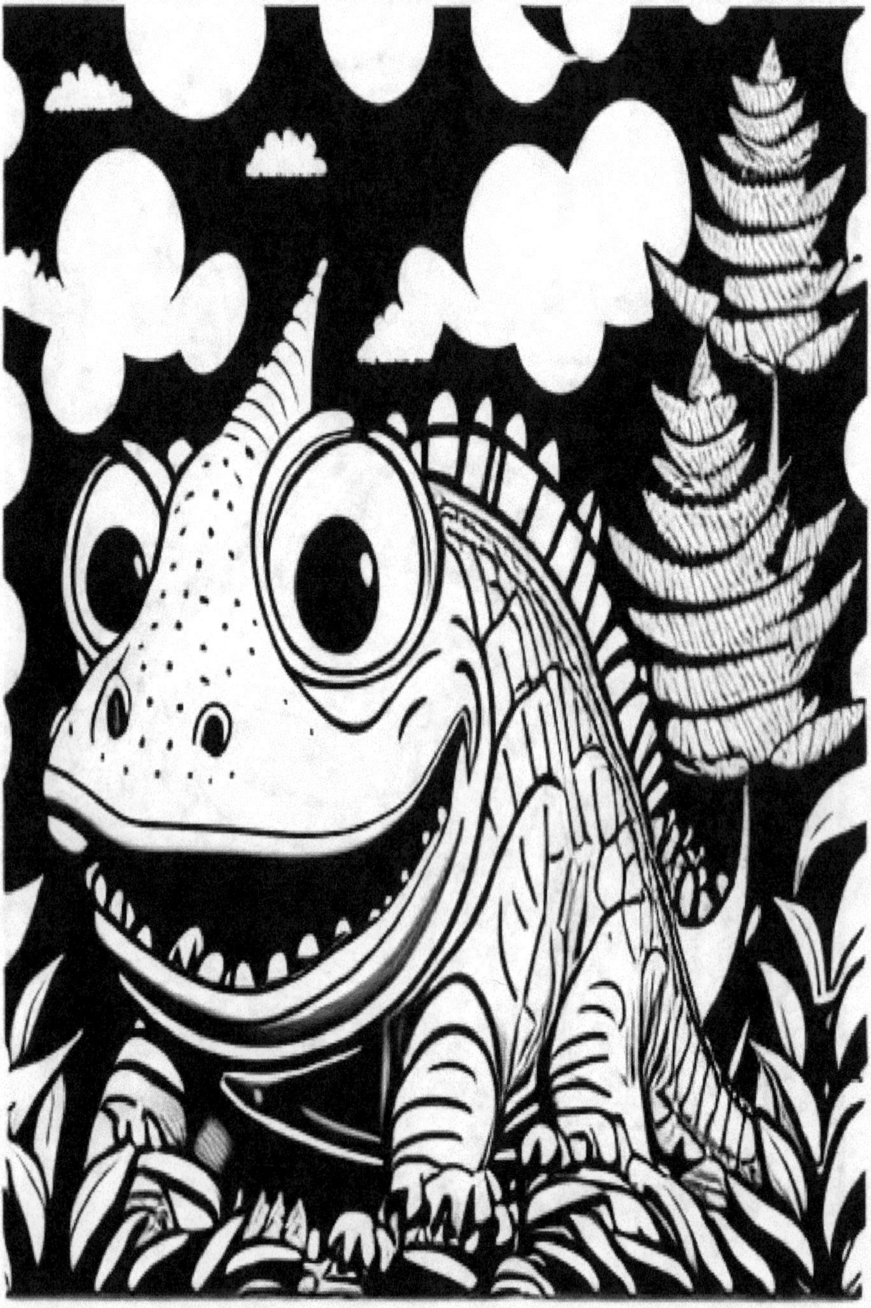

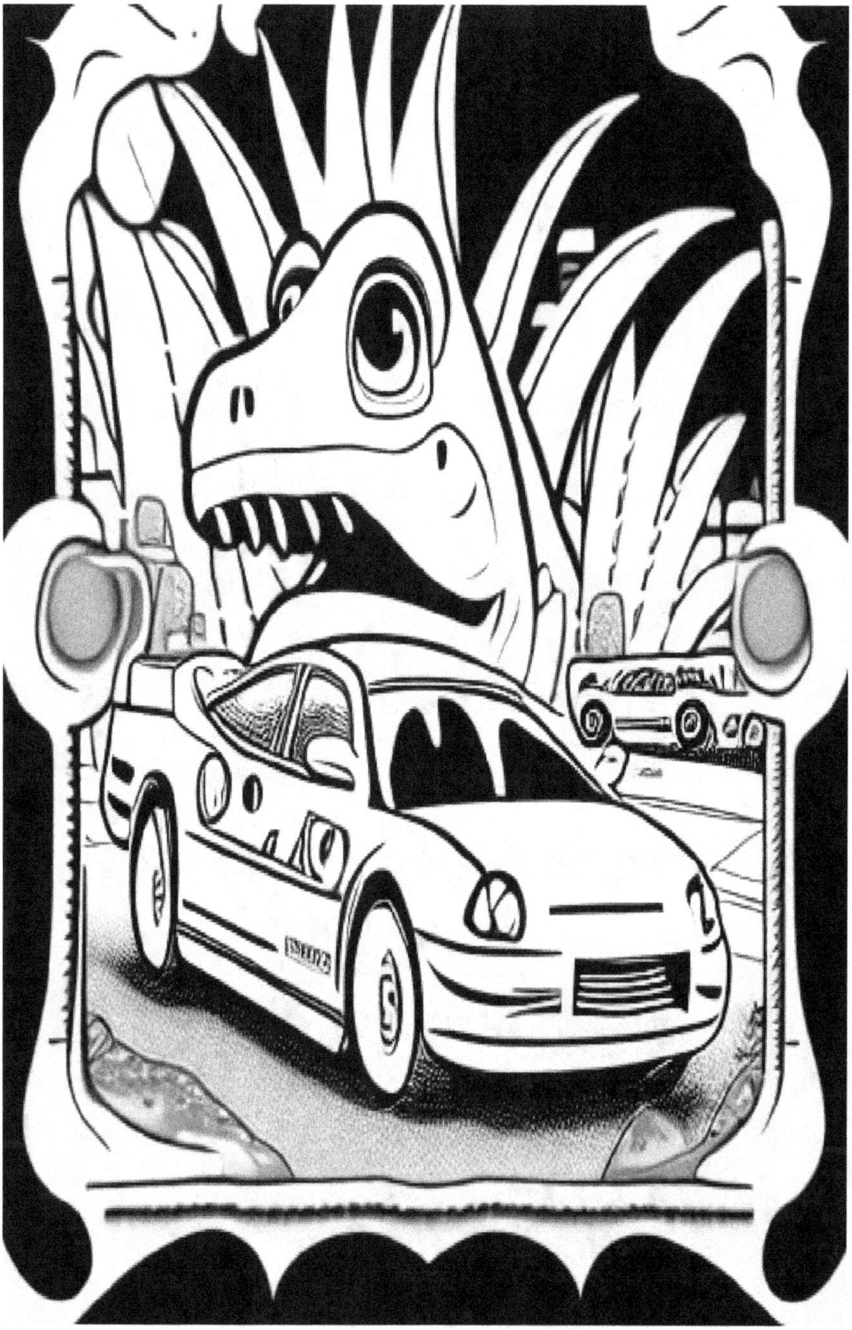

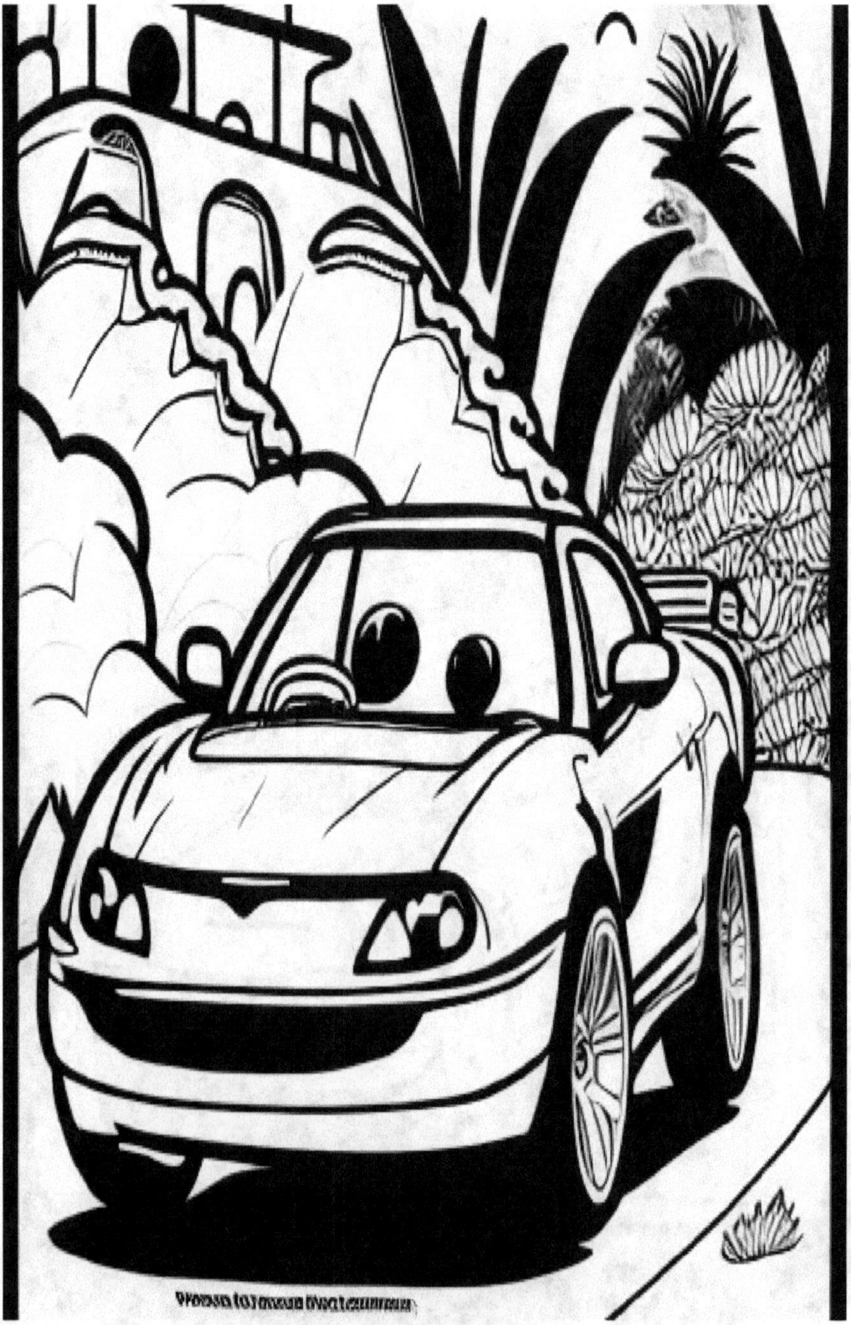

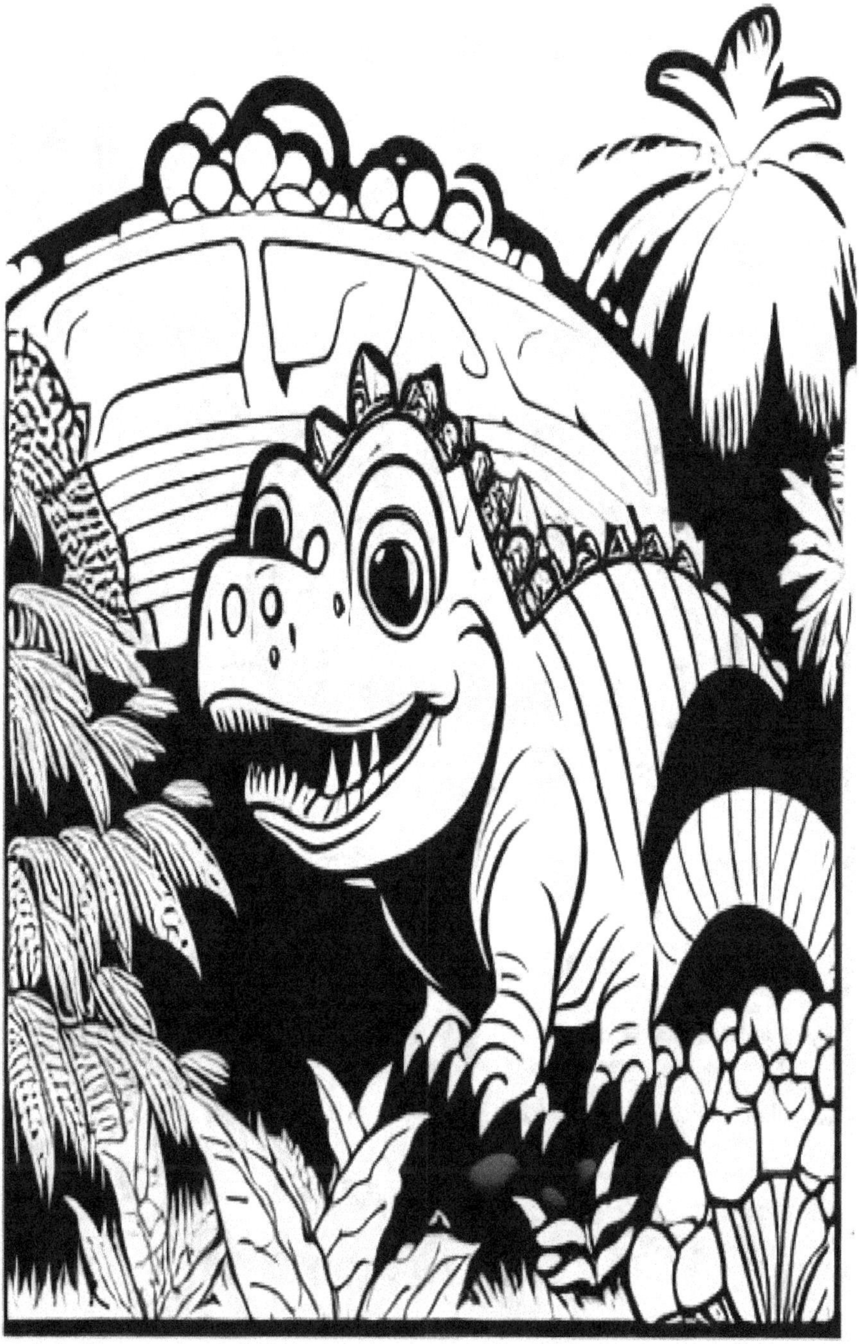

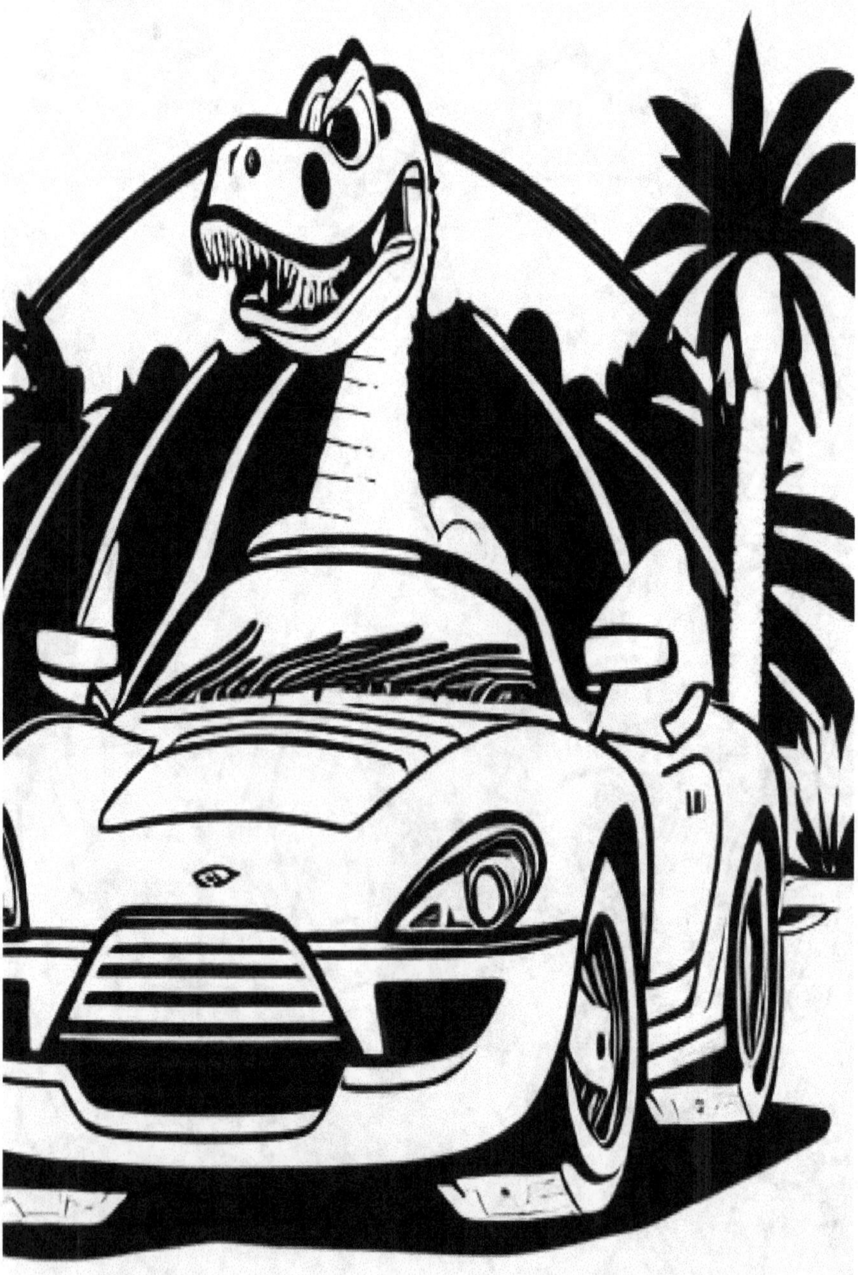

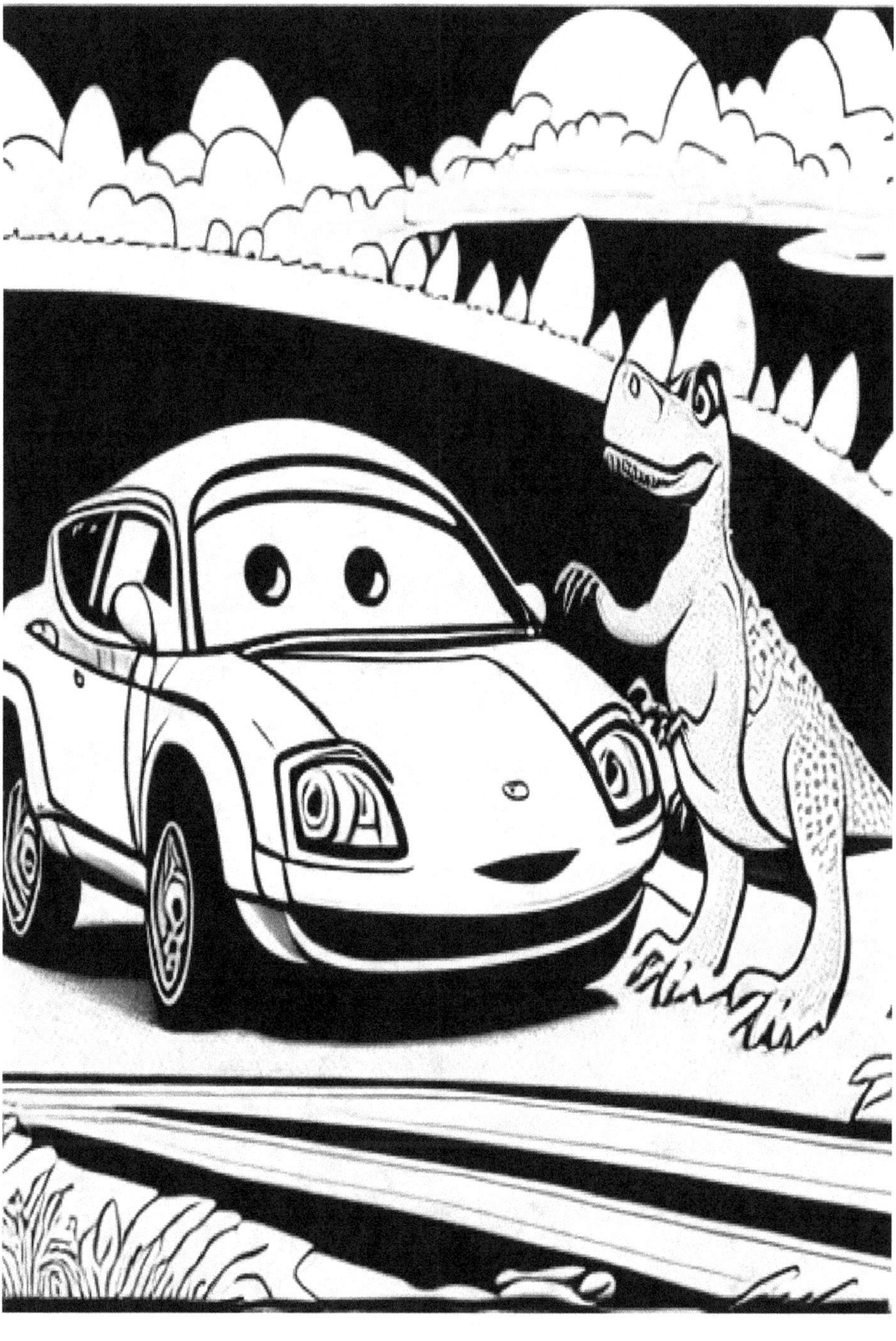

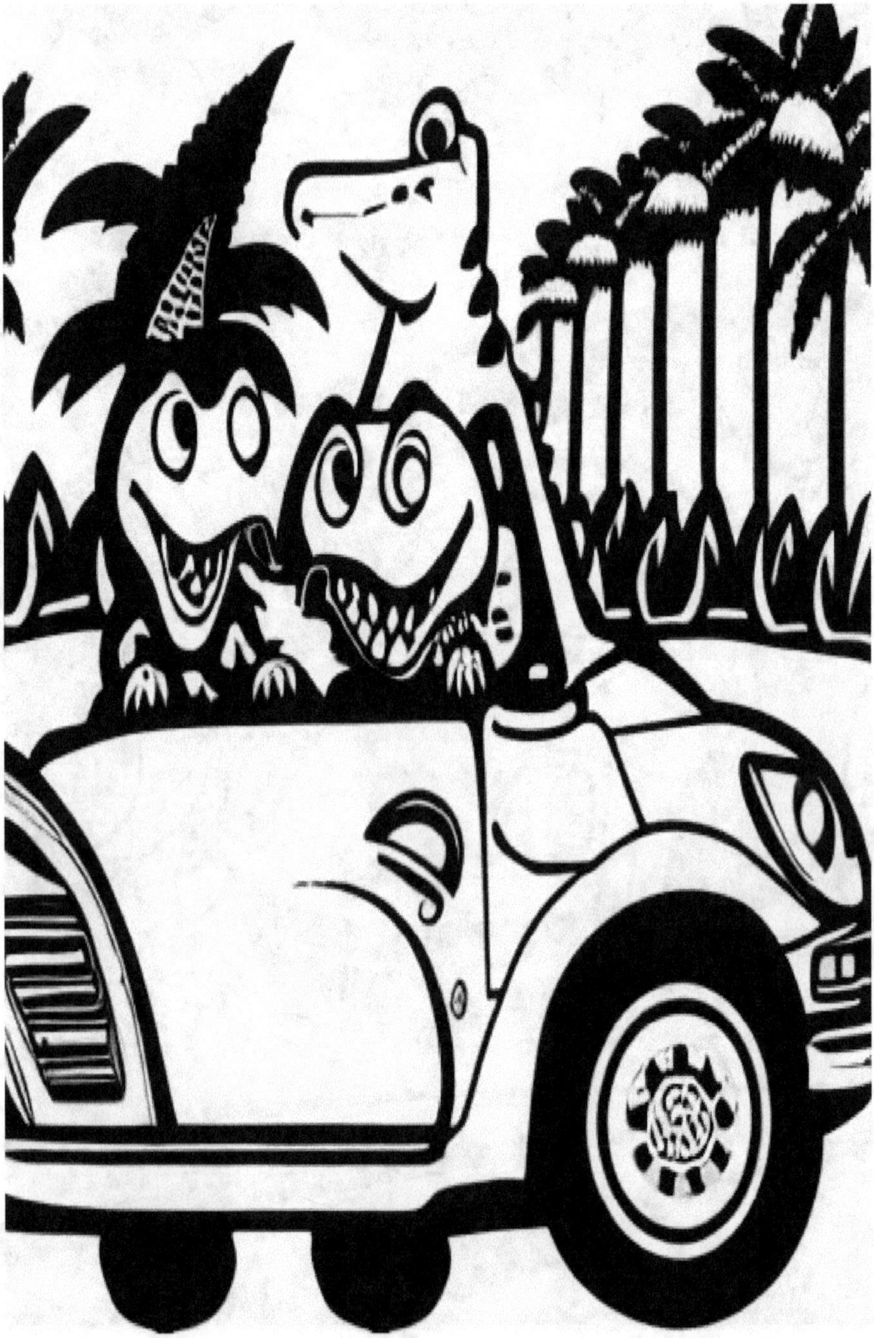

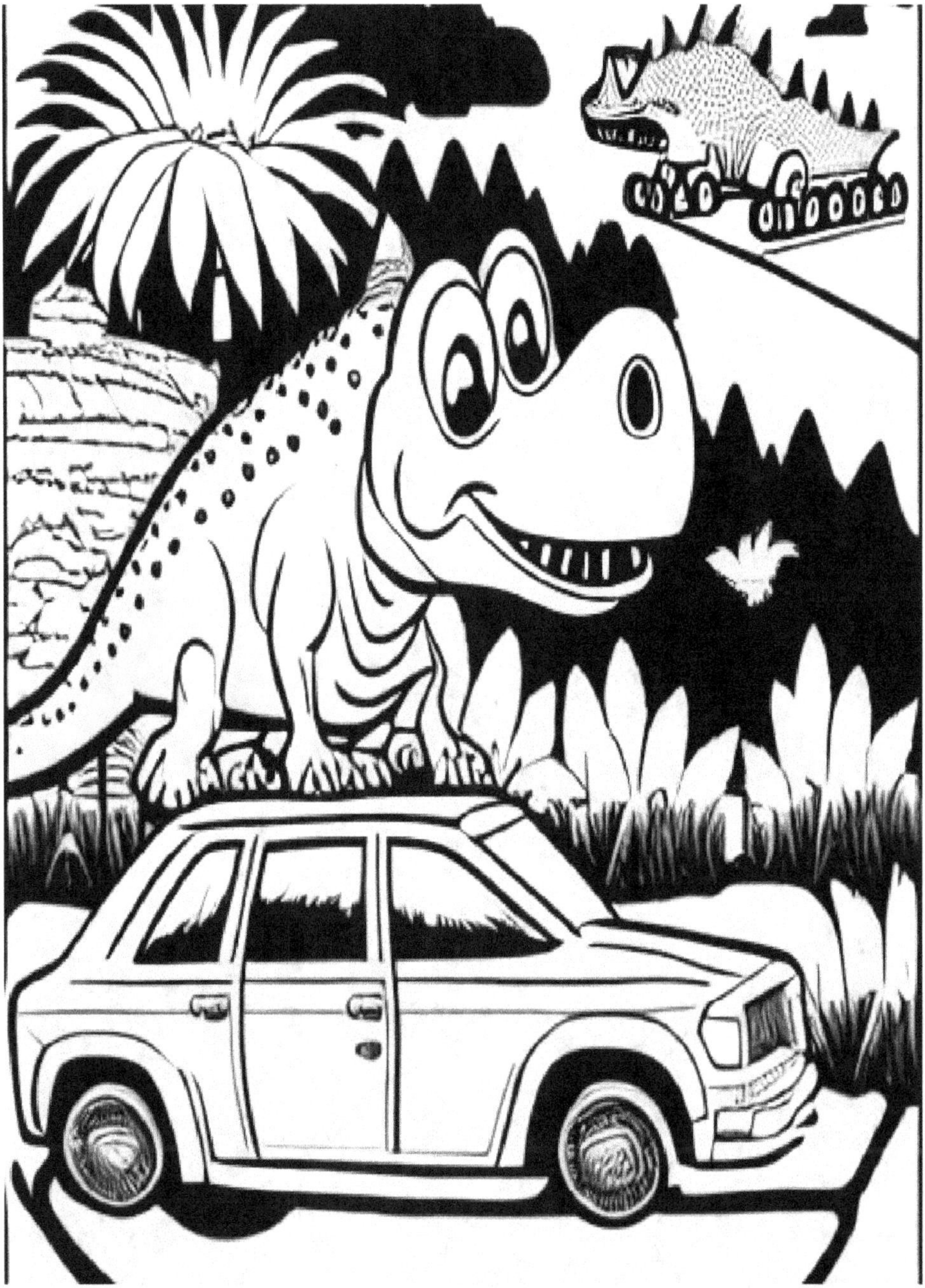

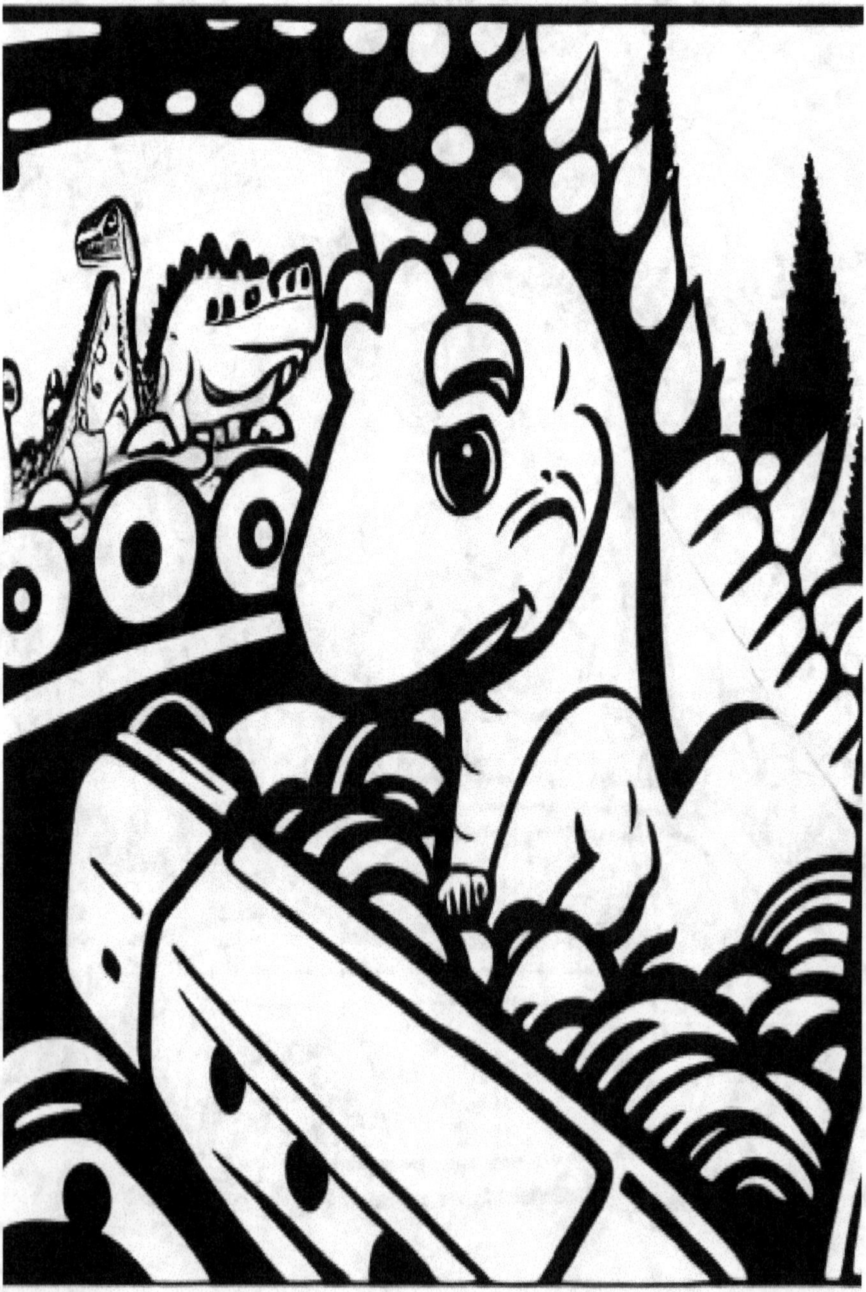

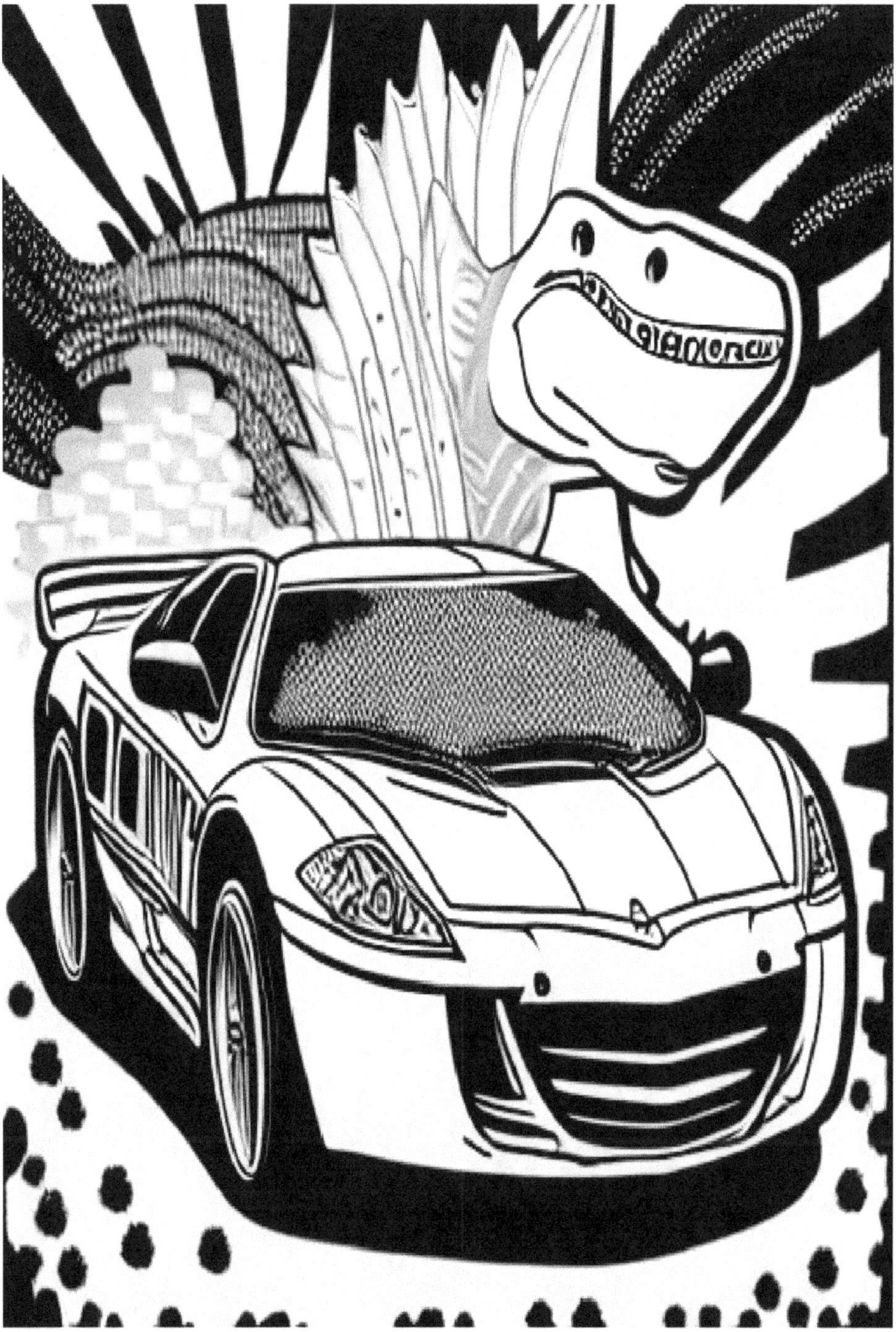

www.ingramcontent.com/pod-product-compliance
Lightning Source LLC
Chambersburg PA
CBHW070438220526
45466CB00004B/1728
* 9 7 9 8 3 9 8 1 1 5 8 6 4 *